Praise for **The Green Foodprint**

Linda Riebel offers her readers a highly accessible and judgment-free book that helps newcomers to the world of sustainable food with easy-to-follow guidelines. Whether your motivation is saving the planet, improving your health, or just eating in line with your values, this book will help you get there.

> *Michele Simon, JD, MPH, Author of Appetite for Profit: How the Food Industry Undermines Our Health and How to Fight Back*

In today's complex world, even eating is a political act. In *The Green Foodprint*, Linda Riebel explains where our food comes from, why it matters and what we can do about it. This concise, comprehensive and easy-to-read resource helps guide us towards healthier choices and a more sustainable future.

> *Buzz Hofford, District Manager, Bon Appétit Management Company, and owner, Sustainable Foods Network*

My patients want to know how to improve their diets to support their recovery from breast cancer, but don't have the time or energy to dig through all the latest information about food, health, and the environment. This book gives them what they need, whatever their individual requirements may be. *The Green Foodprint* will go on the recommended reading list for my patients.

> *Lyn Freeman, Ph.D., Director of Mind Matters Research*

The Green Foodprint shows that you can personally tackle global warming from the dinner table—and feel healthier while doing it.

> *Laura Stec, Chef and author of Cool Cuisine: Taking the Bite Out of Global Warming*

We are the privileged who can choose what to eat every day. This luxury comes with the responsibility of choosing food that benefits our bodies and our planet. *The Green Foodprint* provides the information you need to make informed and humane food decisions—it will empower you with important knowledge and practical tips that will help you make a difference.

> *Mark Berman, MD*

D0395296

Unlike so many other books about trying to save the planet through our food choices, this book understands that not everyone is ready to become a vegan. With options to choose plant-based foods when we can and to cook more of our own food when we can, Linda Riebel offers a path out of complacency, regardless of where we are with our own preferences. Add this one by Linda Riebel to the favorites shelf if you want to do your share to slow down the planetary degradation and be part of the solution.

Patti Breitman, co-author of How to Eat Like a Vegetarian Even If You Never Want to Be One

The Green Foodprint is a wonderful little book, packed full of powerful yet simple advice on how to make the best food choices for oneself and the planet. It is also extremely easy to read, with lots of short sections, lists, and true stories. The best thing about this book, and what makes it unique (in my experience), is that it gives readers a wide variety of options to choose from so they can make their food choices earth-friendly. The focus of the book is on the good news—on solutions that are already well established and that are practical and often simple. I highly recommend this book to anyone who wants to learn how they can eat more healthfully while also helping to save our planet.

Melanie Joy, Ph.D., author of Why We Love Dogs, Eat Pigs, and Wear Cows

The Green Foodprint is a remarkable book that can change how we think and live—and definitely how we eat. The author, Dr. Linda Riebel, is a longtime scholar and activist in this area. Dr. Riebel gives us crisp practical advice in highly readable sections brimming with interest, humor, color, and memorable examples. Here is a book we should all read and read again.

Ruth Richards, MD, Ph.D., editor of Everyday Creativity and New Views of Human Nature

The Green Foodprint

Food Choices for Healthy People and a Healthy Planet

By Linda Riebel, Ph.D.

𝕋P

Print and Pixel Books

Lafayette, California

Published by Print and Pixel Books, an imprint of Cosmick Press
Lafayette, California

Riebel, Linda. *The Green Foodprint: Food Choices for Healthy People and a
Healthy Planet*

ISBN: 978-0-9833051-1-8

Second Edition, 2011.
The first edition of this book (2010) was titled *The Earth-Friendly Food Chain:
Food Choices for a Living Planet.*

This book may be ordered from Amazon.com, Barnesandnoble.com,
Printandpixelbooks.com, and from Print and Pixel Books, POB 1397,
Lafayette CA, 94549.

Printed and bound in the United States of America.

Cover design by Elysa Lozano
Typesetting by Jill Ronsley, Sun Editing & Book Design

All of the author's profits from this book go to SaveNature.org.

Publisher's Cataloging-in-Publication data

Riebel, Linda.
    The green foodprint : food choices for healthy people and a healthy planet / by
Linda Riebel, Ph.D.
        p. cm.
        ISBN : 978-0-9833051-1-8
        Includes bibliographical references and index.

1. Natural foods --Health aspects --United States. 2. Natural foods
--Environmental aspects. 3. Sustainable living --United States. 4. Local foods
--United States. 5. Food supply. 6. Sustainable agriculture --United States. 7.
Natural foods --Purchasing. 8. Food consumption --North America. I. Title.

TX369 .R42 2011
641.5/63 --dc22

*To all the people who are working to create
the sustainable new food economy,
this book is gratefully dedicated.*

Contents

Foreword

It took about 165,000 years of human history on planet Earth for the human population to reach one billion. It took only 130 years for the second billion. That number was reached in 1930.

Thirty years later, in 1960, there were three billion of us.

Fourteen years later, in 1974, there were four billion.

Thirteen years later, in 1987, there were five billion.

Twelve years later, in 1999, there were six billion.

As our numbers have increased, of course, so has our collective impact on the environment and on other people. Today, there are about one trillion pounds of human flesh on the planet. Now, as never before in human history, we must take responsibility for our global footprint. If we don't learn to walk lightly on the Earth, to tread gently and to live within the planet's means, the outcome will be disastrous. We shall perish.

In this light, all of our choices and ways of life need to be reexamined, and none more urgently than our food choices.

This is because our food choices, in particular, can either defile the Earth and the life it holds, or they can help to protect and preserve the viability of the biosphere and the wellbeing of the whole Earth community. Yet how do we know what the ecological and social implications are of our choices? How do we know what happens across the long food chains that bring nourishment to our tables?

It would certainly be helpful if some trustworthy and thoughtful researcher would explore these questions in real depth, and then to present us with clear, accurate, and practical guidelines. Linda Riebel has done precisely that.

In *The Green Foodprint,* she lights our way to living with respect for ourselves and the Earth, for making food choices that bring us both greater personal health and also greater planetary health. There is excellent counsel in this book.

Follow its advice and you will be making a statement to others that will be heard loud and clear. The Earth matters. Your life matters. Your choices matter. Linda Riebel shows you how to make your dining experiences congruent with your love for this Earth and for the all the many living beings who, like us humans, call it home.

—John Robbins

Acknowledgements

I want to thank John Robbins, for inspiring me and millions of other people to bring consciousness and humanity to our food choices; Ken Jacobsen, for his ideas, his friendship, and his unflagging faith in this project; Melanie Joy, Ph.D., for thoughtful and valuable feedback; Michael Greger, MD, of the Humane Society of the United States, for his insight into factory farming; Andy Snow, science teacher and avid gardener; Michele Simon, JD, for being a tireless defender of eaters' rights; Ruth Richards, MD, Ph.D., creativity expert and colleague at Saybrook University; Michael Larsen and Elizabeth Pomada, for all they have taught me about publishing; Rakhi Rao and Pete Elman of Print and Pixel Books; Sandra Gary for detailed editing; Jill Ronsley for layout; my colleagues at Sustainable Lafayette, who have set the standard for transforming a town to sustainability, especially Steve Richard, Rebecca Calahan Klein, Janet Thomas, and Michael Dawson; Norm Gershenz at SaveNature.Org, for helping link our food choices to the mission of saving precious ecosystems; and for so many reasons, my husband, Brad Wade.

Author's Note

This book was written by a psychologist who became an environmental teacher and writer. The transition began when I visited Uganda with a group of friends to visit the rare mountain gorillas and other wild animals in that country's splendid rainforests. When I learned about the "bushmeat trade" (people kill wild animals and eat them), I wanted to run outside, stop people in the streets, and cry, "Don't do it! Don't kill the chimps and the water bucks and the colobus monkeys!"

But I had no right. Many of these people were hungry. And as every good therapist knows, you don't ask other people to do what you have not done yourself. I came home and decided to learn about America's food system. I enlisted a co-author and together we sought out evidence on all sides of a debate. We read the beef industry website, books from committed vegetarians, critics of the meat industry, and medical research. We contacted EPA scientists, farmers, and professors of agriculture. We read newspapers, industry reports, and government publications. I attended conferences held by environmentalists, business leaders, and farmers.

The result was the 2002 book *Eating to Save the Earth*. I became an advocate for the new food movement, speaking at churches, schools, and conferences, and helping to create the sustainability program at Saybrook University in San Francisco, where I have been a faculty member since 1993. I joined the board of a nonprofit that saves rainforests and another that works to transform my town into a model of green living. One day when I was preparing handouts to give at a talk, the word "foodprint" emerged as a typo. What a perfect word for the idea of healing our food footprint! Or perhaps it was the author's creative unconscious. Other people have independently invented the term, and I hope we use it to guide us to a healthier food world.

In my 25 years as a psychotherapist, I worked mostly with people who had eating disorders, and saw first-hand how eating can become an all-purpose coping strategy—and how it backfires, creating unhappiness, overweight, or poor health. Some of the things I learned about suffering, change, and healing on an individual level apply to society at large. For instance, almost every problem started out as a solution. Eating as a comfort for sadness eased the sadness. It worked for a while, so people kept doing it. Putting chemicals on plants to kill bugs improved crop yields. It worked for a while, so people kept doing it. Now the disadvantages (overweight from overeating, pollution and illness from pesticides) outweigh the payoffs, and we have a choice: we can keep doing it, or we can change.

I used to tell my therapy clients, "This habit has done all it can for you. You've given it a fair test." Framing their trouble not as a moral failing but as an outdated solution released their guilt, helping them to give up their problem at last. To reinforce my point, I would sometimes add, "What parts of your life so far do you want to carry with you into the future?"

Industrial agriculture, treating nature as the enemy to be defeated with machines and chemicals, sounded like a good idea at the time. It paid off at first and we reaped the advantages of abundant, cheap food. We've given it a fair test–over a century, with all the government subsidies, university research, capital, and lack of regulation that the biggest industry enthusiast could have ever desired.

But it's time to change. The disadvantages of the destructive engine of industrial agriculture have become clear. We're now at the stage of choosing what parts of our food system we want to carry with us into the future.

I'm happy to say that much of the news is encouraging. *The Green Foodprint* chronicles the progress, distills green food choices into five easy-to-remember guidelines, and shares stories of the people and organizations that are working to make our food world healthy, safe, and sustainable for all.

Preface

Your food footprint, like your carbon footprint, reflects how much of Earth's resources go to support you. You can easily reduce your foodprint.

- Every time you choose food with less packaging, you are saving trees and other materials.
- Every meal without meat reduces the use of pesticides, antibiotics, hormones, water, and land, freeing more land to grow food for hungry people.
- Every organic egg represents cleaner food, more humane treatment of animals, and an investment in the healthier new food economy.

Our food sector is enormous—over $1 trillion in 2009, more than the total gross domestic product of many countries. In 2008, the average American's food bill amounted to $2,577. As sustainable business guru Paul Hawken says, "The cash register is the daily voting booth in democratic capitalism." This book shows you how to make your votes—all 2,577 of them—count.

And it's getting easier all the time. Millions of citizens have made it clear that they want healthy food that does not harm the environment. Inventive farmers and distributors are working hard to supply it. Best of all, choices that are better for human health are almost always better for the planet.

Your share of this cornucopia depends, of course, on your circumstances. Are you on a tight budget or feeding a young family? Then you might be spending your food dollars on basics, with an occasional splurge. Are you a business executive who takes colleagues to lunch at restaurants on expense account several times a week? Your food dollars are spent very differently. With so many possible lifestyles, there's no average food style. But anyone, of any age or social group, with any combination of needs and preferences, can make food choices that help the Earth.

Like your fingerprint, your green foodprint can be as individual as you are.

I
N
T
R
O

Introduction:
An Earth-Friendly Food Chain

O F ALL THE ECONOMIC sectors that need to be revamped in the 21st century, food is high on the list. Only cars and other forms of transportation cause more environmental damage than our food system. In this section, I'll explain why—and what we can do about it.

> Like those big Industrial Age factories that once billowed black smoke, American agriculture is mired in a mind-set that relies on capital, chemistry, and machines.
>
> — Chef and author Dan Barber

How Can Food Be a Problem?

Imagine knowing that your food came to you in a way that was safe and life-affirming for you, and for the farmworkers, the land, water, and all creatures involved. It would be an Earth-friendly food chain.

But our current system of growing, processing, and distributing food is dangerous, long, and destructive.

- Pesticides, fertilizers, and other chemicals used to produce food foul our rivers and end up in the oceans, causing hundreds of "dead zones" around the world.
- Rainforests in Indonesia and South America are being cut down (or worse, burned down) to produce soybeans, beef, and palm oil for Americans. Seventy percent of previously forested land in the Amazon is occupied by cattle pastures, and crops for animal feed cover a large part of the remainder.
- The U.S. is losing topsoil ten times faster than the natural replenishment rate, and the soil that is left is often depleted of nutrients from overuse and erosion.

The prospect of 5 billion people eating the way Americans do is an ecological impossibility, requiring more grain than the world can grow and more energy, water, and land than the world can supply.

—Alan Durning, founder,
Northwest Environment Watch

Food manufacture and climate change

Many of the problems caused by industrial agriculture stem from *monoculture*, which means growing huge fields of the same crop in the same location. Monoculture sounds sensible, bringing to farming the efficiency that works so well in manufacturing.

Unfortunately, in nature it backfires. Monoculture exhausts the soil, so farmers use more chemical fertilizers. Those vast amber waves of grain also attract bugs with an immense supply of their favorite food. Science writer Janine Benyus calls monoculture an "all-you-can-eat restaurant for pests." So growers use more pesticides, creating an arms race between humans and other creatures—an endless game of crops and robbers. Meanwhile, 1,100 United States food species or varieties are endangered or threatened with extinction; others have already disappeared. Even if a species survives, inbreeding leads to what experts call a "genetic bottleneck."

This is not very wise of us. Ecologist Kenny Ausubel says, "Biodiversity—the sum total of all the world's life forms, organisms, and genes—is nature's fail-safe mechanism against extinction. Any smart banker will recommend a diversified portfolio to hedge against a risk."

Consider all the species of animals and organisms involved in a single field. Soil organisms and field animals also benefit from crops. Bacteria feed on the cellulose fibers of straw that farmers return to the soil. Amoebas feed on bacteria, making lignite fibers available for uptake by plants. Algae provide organic matter and serve as natural nitrogen fixers. Moles and gophers bore under the fields, aerating the soil and improving its water-holding capacity. Spiders, centipedes and insects grind organic matter from the surface soil and leave behind enriched droppings. Earthworms provide aeration and fertilizer, and maintain soil structure. By contrast, industrial farming techniques compact and contaminate the soil, depriving these diverse organisms of food sources and instead assaulting them with chemicals, destroying the basis of soil fertility.

Our tiny helpers

We would starve without birds, bats, and bees to pollinate the crops we depend on. Bees give services valued at $15 billion annually—but they're dying. Whole colonies of bees are simply abandoning their

3

hives. Over the last 30 years, over half of the bee colonies that pollinate California's $1 billion almond industry have been lost. Besides the virus-fungus combination that is so deadly to them, they have to contend with pollution, pesticides, mites, and mite-killing chemicals. Current farming practices don't help. For instance, almond trees are grown on cleared land, so there are no wild flowers for bees to live on; growers have to rent bees brought in from hundreds or even thousands of miles away to pollinate the trees. So stress from being shipped adds to the bees' problems. Pollutants are destroying the fragrances in flowers, making it harder for pollinators to find the blossoms and pollinate crops.

If we kill off all the bees, bats, and birds, who will pollinate our food crops? We have already exterminated so many fish off our coasts that some fishing zones have been closed. Do we literally intend to eat ourselves out of house and planet?

The real solution

Though the numbers aren't perfect, we know that the answer is to save habitats, consume less, and reduce overpopulation. Fortunately, solutions to these problems are already in place. This book shows you how, using the Earth-friendly food chain, you can help the planet and yourself, every day.

Nature bats last—and owns the stadium.

—Amory Lovins, L. Hunter Lovins,
and Paul Hawken,
authors of *Natural Capitalism*

Good News for the Earth

We have reason to be cautiously hopeful about our future. People in many fields are inventing or reviving ways to live lightly on the Earth, and citizens are demanding green goods and services. Thousands of non-profit organizations around the world work to restore the earth and create social justice. The socially responsible investing market is worth $3 trillion in 2010. Schoolchildren are sending money to save rain forests, architects are designing energy-efficient homes and offices, religious communities are adopting Earth-friendly causes, and manufacturers are streamlining their processes. Exciting developments are taking place all around us—including in our food world.

- The U.S. organic market has grown 20% per year, to nearly $6 billion, and there are now over 6,000 farmers' markets nationwide, a 16% increase in one year.
- Conservation tilling methods reduced soil erosion by 43% between 1982 and 2003.
- There are 1,667 land trusts nationwide that protect farmland from development.

In this book, you will find dozens more stories of environmental good news. Maybe you, too, will have a creative idea that will become part of this great moment in history.

Surprising partnerships

Cooperation is occurring between unlikely partners. For instance, the Blue Green Alliance, founded in 2006 by United Steelworkers and the Sierra Club, convinces business to go green, protects workers' rights, and shows workers that there are jobs in the green economy. With membership of labor unions and environmental organizations, Blue Green Alliance now represents 13 million members.

- North Carolina has 8,000 open-air cesspools (which can contaminate watersheds) because the hog industry creates more waste than the cities of New York, Los Angeles, Chicago, and Houston combined. Environmental Defense partnered with Frontline Farmers, a group of pork producers, to halt construction of more cesspools and to turn the waste into fertilizer.

- Between 1990 and 2004, more than 100,000 acres of grazing land in California were urbanized. To protect what's left, the California Rangeland Conservation Coalition—a partnership of ranchers and conservationists—works to preserve woodlands and grazing land.

Such partnerships can be found in many unexpected places. In Texas, small farmers, the Central Texas Cattlemen's Association, the U.S. Army, and Environmental Defense are partnering to protect land at Fort Hood.

It's encouraging that people are reaching across old divides to work together.

Big business gets the message

Big business and nature groups are finding common cause. U.S. Climate Action Partnership (USCAP) combines major environmental groups and major corporations to tackle climate change. USCAP includes some of the world's largest corporations, with combined revenues of $2 trillion and 2.7 million workers in all 50 states and many other countries.

Walmart hired the former president of the Sierra Club to oversee its environmental initiatives. With more than 1.4 million employees, 127 million customer visits a week in its 4,000 stores, and $351 billion in revenue, Walmart is bigger than the economies of 160 nations. Environmental Defense is helping Walmart address global warming, alternative fuel, packaging, and sustainable seafood. Simply by turning off engines while trucks are being loaded, the company reduced emissions equivalent to taking 20,000 cars off the road.

Cities doing their share

Seattle, which already recycles 44% of its trash, has added mandatory food scrap recycling. Lafayette, California, collects all food waste, even meat, bones, coffee grounds and filters, soiled napkins, and paper plates. In France, the city of Lille fuels its 100 buses using biogas fuel made from household food scraps, yard clippings, weeds, and flowers, expecting to convert over 100 tons of green waste a year.

The power of one and the power of many

High school biology teacher Tom Furrer was stumped when a student asked him, "Why are we losing species at such a rapid rate, things that we all love? What can we do?"

That weekend, Furrer happened to encounter a man who was saving a few endangered steelhead trout in a pond in his back yard. Furrer enlisted his students to restore the nearby trout stream and start a fish conservation project. Twenty-five years later, all seven miles of the stream have been restored and the high school's fish project is a fully licensed hatchery. Among the graduates of the program are environmental lawyers, science teachers, a stem cell scientist, and a fish hatchery manager.

Freecycle started in Tucson as an email list by one person and now has over 4,500 local groups with millions of members in 85 countries. When you join this group (free, of course), you get emails about things your neighbors are giving away—clothing, gardening tools, books, exercise machines, food, seeds, toys, and much more. You can get free stuff and give away your unneeded things to someone who will use them. The freecycle web site claims, "We are currently keeping over 500 tons a day out of landfills. This amounts to five times the height of Mt. Everest in the past year alone, when stacked in garbage trucks." I don't know how they got this statistic, but I like the image.

Friends of the Earth/Middle East is an organization of Israeli, Jordanian, and Palestinian environmentalists who work together to clean up the Jordan River and the Dead Sea. This organization also promotes healthy food, solar energy, and eco-tourism.

This widespread support of Earth-friendly choices may come as a surprise. You may have thought people who care about the environment were just a few earnest activists holding meetings and criticizing other people's lifestyles. Or you may be an environmentally concerned citizen worried that there aren't enough like-minded people. In fact, researchers have found what they call a New Green Mainstream, over 50 million people who make decisions every day based on environmental concern.

Steward of the land

Nash Huber was given the Steward of the Land Award by the American Farmland Trust. Huber and his wife Patty McManus farm over 400 sustainably managed organic acres in Sequim, Washington, growing over 100 types of produce. The farm composts material from nearby dairy farms and their own vegetable fields. Through grassroots organizations, they have saved hundreds of acres of nearby farmland and wildlife habitat and participated in projects to help salmon, plant buffers near creeks, and improve water quality.

What's next?

As these groups and individuals show, great strides have been made. But we're not out of the woods. Human demands on the planet's natural resources have tripled since 1961. World population continues to grow faster than the Earth can support. Some industries like things just the way they are and obstruct change. Others make empty gestures or engage in greenwash (claiming more environmental virtue than they have).

On the individual level, there's a gap between what people say they are willing to do for the Earth, and what they actually do. This book will help you close that gap and join others who are saving the Earth with their food choices.

Technology—Boon or Bane?

In the 1960s, some modern inventions (pesticides, herbicides, new irrigation methods, and machines) were exported to hungry countries to ease the food crises they were facing. This "Green Revolution" was meant to bring the blessing of modern technology to people in need. But over time, the Green Revolution backfired. Countries that adopted it are plagued by soil erosion, land pollution, and water shortages, plus more stillbirths, lowered sperm counts, and cancer. Says R.K. Mahajan, agricultural economist at India's Punjabi University, "The Green Revolution is not as green as it was earlier—it has now become brown and pale."

Today there is another wave of clever inventions intended to ease food shortages and environmental damage. Can they be trusted?

I am enthusiastic about some of these inventions: GPS (global positioning system) helps farmers direct water to the parts of their fields that need it most. Such "precision agriculture" can also help reduce overuse of fertilizers and other chemicals. The Fair Tracing Project will let shoppers check whether the farmer who grew the produce was fairly compensated. Another internet tool (Aid Matrix) helps distribute surplus food to the hungry, reducing waste. And if scientists succeed in their project to grow meat cells in vitro, the suffering of billions of animals could be eliminated.

The scoop on poop

A research farm in Sterksel, the Netherlands, burns hog manure, captures the methane, and turns it into electricity. Most of the electricity is sold to the local utility; leftover waste becomes fertilizer, which releases less carbon dioxide than synthetic fertilizer. This process also saves $190,000 a year in waste disposal fees. Meanwhile, in the U.S., the EPA has teamed with USDA and U.S. Department of Energy to capture methane from manure and turn it into electricity. In 2009, 150 of these systems produced 374,000 mega-watt hours of energy.

African countries on the Atlantic coast are using satellite surveillance to catch poachers and pirates. Winemakers in California are installing solar panels in their vineyards, "bottling sunshine in more ways than one," as one reporter wrote. Recycling rates have jumped tenfold in some East Coast cities since RecycleBank started rewarding homeowners for recycling.

Other inventions I am wary of. Irradiating meat to protect it from contamination or spoiling is merely putting a Band-Aid on dirty slaughtering practices. Genetically modifying corn so it can withstand the onslaught of pesticides just permits the use of more pesticides. Inserting features of one species into another (anchovy genes into orange juice, for instance) will surely have unintended consequences.

Traditional techniques

Meanwhile, ancient methods are being rediscovered.

- Rotating crops and letting land rest ("lie fallow") so that the soil does not get exhausted.
- Using friendly bugs to eliminate bugs we don't like.
- Putting chickens into pastures to recycle cow pats and scratch the dirt, loosening the soil.

11

Ancient methods of moving and storing water are being revived. Stone-lined underground aqueducts in Syria have been restored, providing water for fruit and nut trees. Ancient irrigation networks have been revived in Peru and Italy. Foot-powered pumps of a kind designed in China 2,000 years ago are being provided to farmers in southern Africa. Other traditional water collection and storage methods are being revived in India.

Solving a gas problem

Cow burps have been in the news, and they're not funny. They contain methane, a greenhouse gas that is far more dangerous than carbon dioxide, and if you add up all the cows in the world, their burps add up to a serious environmental hazard. Taking the problem by the horns, Penn State University dairy scientist Alexander Hristov created an oregano-based supplement that reduced cows' methane emissions by 40%. If early trials are successfully repeated, this could reduce the damage done by innocent cows.

The best of both

Genetic modification of living things is risky—but there are safer ways of harnessing genetic knowledge to improve breeds. *Marker-assisted selection* combines the modern science of genetics with old-fashioned cross-breeding to increase crop yields. Scientists select individual plants with desirable traits by scanning their genes, and then use traditional cross-breeding of these selected plants to pass on those traits. This method shows it is possible to harness human ingenuity without unleashing forces we don't fully understand. Sustainable agriculture, which is a collection of old and new methods, combines the best of both worlds.

Four Birds on One Branch:
Many Good Results from One Action

Yossi Leshem, an Israeli bird expert and director of the International Center for the Study of Bird Migration, was troubled by the deaths of hundreds of birds in northern Israel. The birds were being killed by the chemicals used to eradicate the rats that were eating the farmers' crops. Leshem persuaded a kibbutz to try a different solution. Barn owl boxes were installed to lure owls to make their homes at the kibbutz, and within a few years the rat problem was solved. An Ohio Jewish community group gave funds so the kibbutz members could donate building materials for owl nesting boxes to their Jordanian neighbors. Little by little, overcoming obstacles, the project is helping former enemies reach out to one another.

In the food transformation now under way, we can accomplish three or four or even more goals with a single food choice. For example, choosing more fresh fruits and vegetables reduces wasteful packaging and processing—and offers better nutrition. Eating food produced locally offers many advantages, as you can see by this list.

Locally Grown Food

- Money stays in your community
- Reduces use of refrigerants and packaging
- More likely to be organic
- Less gasoline used for transportation
- Saves family farms
- Preserves alternatives to industrial monopolies.

Here is another process that has many positive results:

Organically Produced Eggs

- More humane treatment of animals
- Chickens are fed a vegetarian diet (natural for them)
- No antibiotics
- No pesticides in the hens' food.

Each positive consequence has happy consequences of its own: No pesticides in hens' food means less pollution in the creeks near chicken farms; this allows fish to survive. It also increases the market share of organic food for the hens. Just as there are damaging ripple effects of industrial agriculture, there are helpful ripple effects in the new food economy.

The following actions have the most numerous happy consequences:

- Eat more organic food.
- Eat more locally grown food.
- Eat less meat.
- Eat less fish.
- Grow some of your own food.

Which one of these gives the greatest number of happy consequences? You'll find the answer later in this book.

PART

I

PART I
Your Five Most Important Decisions

With five key food choices, you can create your green foodprint.

- Choose more organic foods.
- Eat lower on the food chain.
- Choose more locally grown food.
- Eat a greater variety of food.
- Create less packaging, processing, and waste.

Decide which recommendations make the most sense for you. If you opt to keep meat in your diet, you can change the kind and amount of meat you eat. If you're a vegetarian or vegan, you can increase your purchase of organics, reduce packaging, and add variety. There's an endless range of options that you can tailor to your lifestyle.

> Ecological restoration is extraordinarily simple: You remove whatever prevents the system from healing itself.
>
> — Paul Hawken, author of *Blessed Unrest*

Eat Food, Not Chemicals

Modern agriculture drenches food in chemicals: pesticides to kill insects, herbicides to kill weeds, and antibiotics for cows, pigs, and chickens. Growers may spray chemicals on a crop repeatedly: once during winter dormancy, again when plants begin to bud, again after flowers are pollinated, and several more times while the crops are growing. Finally, some ripe fruit is sprayed with wax to make it look shiny. Processed food gets additives and preservatives as well.

Yes, I know that everything is made out of chemicals. Water is a chemical, and so is salt. By "chemicals," I mean artificial chemicals used in food production.

The truth about pesticides

Pesticides are poisons intended to kill bugs and other living things that we consider "pests." In this country, nearly a billion pounds of pesticides are applied every year. But over time, pesticides lose power: with short life cycles, insects evolve to become resistant to our poisons faster than we can invent new ones. According to the Pesticide Action Network, the percentage of crops lost to pests has almost doubled since the 1940s, despite an increase in pesticide use.

Farmers, encouraged by chemical manufacturers, respond by using yet more chemicals in what agriculture experts call the "pesticide treadmill." This situation reminds me of drug addiction. When people are addicted, they need ever-greater quantities of the substance to get the same effect. American agriculture seems addicted to chemicals.

These chemicals find their way into our bodies. Over 160 of the active ingredients have been classified by the EPA as known or suspected carcinogens. Even human milk has been contaminated, affecting both industrialized and developing countries. A single dose of pesticides may not be dangerous, but the impact accumulates over a lifetime.

Some chemicals have been banned, but American companies still produce and export them to other nations with less stringent laws. Since we import food from other countries, and only about 1% of imported food is inspected, the chemicals banned here may end up in your body anyway.

Organic—what the USDA labels mean

Fortunately, you can help take these poisons out of circulation by buying organic food.

- "100% organic" means the product is made entirely of organically grown ingredients.
- "Organic" means it is made of at least 95% organic ingredients.
- "Made with organic ingredients" means at least 70% of the ingredients are organic.
- If less than 70% is made of organic ingredients, the food maker may list organic ingredients separately in the information panel.

Organic may appear to be more expensive than conventional, but this is only because industrial agriculture is supported by enormous government subsidies and does not pay for the damage that it causes to human health and the environment. But the health of person and planet is so important that I urge you to consider choosing organic as often as you can.

Can't afford to go all-organic right now? Make these switches first:

Most Important Foods to Buy Organic

Baby food
Milk and butter
Fruits: strawberries, bananas, peaches, cherries, nectarines, apricots, apples, grapes, melons, red raspberries, pears
Vegetables: potatoes, bell peppers, lettuces, spinach, green beans, tomatoes, cucumbers
Protein foods: eggs, seafood, meat, peanut butter
Beverages: coffee, wine
Foods containing soy and corn, to avoid genetically modified food.

Organic farming has many other life-affirming features in addition to avoiding toxic chemicals. The USDA defines it as follows:

- Use of cover crops, green manures [cover crops that are plowed under to improve the soil], animal manures and crop rotations to fertilize the soil, maximize biological activity and maintain long-term soil health.
- Use of biological control, crop rotations and other techniques to manage weeds, insects and diseases.
- An emphasis on biodiversity of the agricultural system and the surrounding environment.
- Using rotational grazing and mixed forage pastures for livestock operations and alternative health care for animal wellbeing.
- Reduction of external and off-farm inputs and elimination of synthetic pesticides and fertilizers and other materials, such as hormones and antibiotics.
- A focus on renewable resources, soil and water conservation, and management practices that restore, maintain and enhance ecological balance.

Organic and health

Conventionally grown fruits and vegetables are bred for high yield, long shelf life, resistance to pests, uniform size, and attractive appearance. Sensible values, to be sure, when produce is shipped thousands of miles, but what about taste and nutrients? Some studies show that fruits and vegetables grown with chemicals are less nutritious than they used to be, and less nutritious than organic. While scientists sort out whether organic growing strengthens the desirable compounds in food, we already know that modern industrial agriculture adds undesirable ones. Chemicals used to grow food include known carcinogens, endocrine disruptors, neurotoxins, and reproductive toxicants. To find out more about these alarming facts, visit whatsonmyfood.org to find out which chemicals were used to grow and process your food.

What you can do:
✓ Buy organic fruits, vegetables, nuts, and grains.
✓ Wash or peel nonorganic produce.
✓ Baked goods, cereals, canned foods are also available in organic form.

Real organic vs greenwash

However, beware of greenwash. Some producers pretend to be green, showing cute animals or green colors in their advertisements and packaging, without making their products sustainable; they hide their real environmental impact; and they fight the prospect of regulation by claiming they will start policing themselves. Some advertising terms are vague and meaningless, such as "eco-friendly" and "natural." To help you assess a corporation, Greenpeace developed four criteria.

• Dirty business. Is the company's core business basically destructive? Using a little solar energy doesn't help if its major business is cutting down forests.

- Ad bluster. If the company's advertising emphasizes a few green products but the company mostly makes destructive ones, that's greenwash.
- Political spin. If the company lobbies against environmental regulations and tries to defeat laws that would help the Earth, while pretending it supports sustainability, that's greenwash.
- "It's the law, stupid!" Claiming credit for actions that are required anyway is greenwash.

How can you know which products are good for the Earth and which are not? Agribusiness corporations constantly pressure regulators to dilute their standards. Sometimes they simply lie—one big dairy processor ignored USDA organic regulations and stalled investigations for years, while labeling its milk organic. To protect our right to know, private groups such as the Institute for Agriculture and Trade Policy iatp.org and Consumers Union greenerchoices.org/eco-labels certify products and foods. The Certified Humane label certifiedhumane.org indicates more humane treatment of animals.

What you can do:
- ✓ Buy green products.
- ✓ Don't be fooled by vague terms (such as "natural") or cuddly pictures and green colors on the labels.
- ✓ Balance hope with skepticism.
- ✓ Get information from watchdog groups, like organicconsumers.org and foodandwaterwatch.org.

Eat Lower on the Food Chain

A food chain is a web showing how living things rely on other living things for their food. Plants turn sunlight and soil nutrients into vegetation; herbivores eat plants; and carnivores eat herbivores (and sometimes other carnivores). Omnivores eat both plants and animals. So animals "higher" on the food chain are consuming life energy that has been concentrated by creatures that they ate "lower" on the chain. There is spirited debate whether humans are by nature omnivores or vegetarians. But there is no debate that the single most powerful choice you can make for the Earth—and to green your foodprint— is to eat "lower" on the food chain by eating less meat, fish, and dairy.

The protein myth

Americans once believed that eating meat three times a day was a sign of worldly success—bacon with breakfast, burger for lunch, roast chicken for dinner. We believed that you risked your health if you didn't eat a lot of meat. In fact, the opposite may be true. The average man actually needs about 60 grams of protein a day (about 2 ounces), and the average woman about 50 grams (about 1½ ounces). And protein comes in nuts, beans, legumes, and some vegetables.

The truth about meat

Meat represents an inefficient use of the food supply because it takes so many pounds of grain and water to produce one pound of beef or pork. Chemicals and pesticides sprayed on the crops grown to feed cattle degrade the soil, and the runoff of these chemicals and pesticides harms oceans, streams, and lakes, injuring or killing the fish and mammals that live there. Then there is loss of biodiversity. Rangeland is cleared for cattle or otherwise degraded by them, destroying the habitats of prairie dogs, wolves, birds, deer, and other animals. Ranchers kill wild animals they believe threaten their herds. Finally, production of meat, milk, and eggs creates more greenhouse gases than cars.

What are we eating?

- Every year, nearly 10 billion land animals are raised and killed in the United States for food.
- Americans eat about 10 billion fish and other sea animals a year. Adding these to land animals, we eat 19,011 animals per minute.

What about hunger?

- 60 to 70% of world's fish catch goes to feed livestock. Every year, 14 million tons of wild-caught fish are fed to pigs and chickens.
- It takes 10 times as much grain to produce the same number of calories of grain-fed beef than if we ate the grain directly.

If all the grain currently fed to livestock in the U.S. was consumed directly by people, the number who could be fed is nearly 800 million.

—David Pimentel, Cornell professor of Ecology and Evolutionary Biology

Greenhouse gases and climate change

Worldwide, farmed animals generate 35-40% of all greenhouse gas methanes, 65% of nitrous oxide, and 64% of ammonia. Reporter Elizabeth Rosenthal calls them "living smokestacks."

Don't drive a cow, man.

Producing two pounds of beef creates more greenhouse gases than driving a car for 3 hours while leaving on all the lights at home. A meat diet produces 3,267 more pounds of carbon dioxide per year than a vegan diet—the emissions difference between driving a Camry sedan and driving a Prius. One study concluded, "The methane that cattle and their manure produce has a global warming effect equal to that of 33 million automobiles."

Water

Beef requires 5 to 10 times as much water per pound to produce as wheat, and 50 times as much as eggs. Plus, animal agriculture is the world's largest source of water pollution.

Manure

Food animals produce 13 times the amount of waste produced by humans. It contains oxygen-depleting substances such as organic matter, ammonia, and pathogens.

- Each dairy cow produces up to 22 tons of waste a year. 1,600 dairies in California's Central Valley produce more waste than a city of 21 million.
- Chicken waste from Arkansas so polluted the rivers that nearby Oklahoma sued the Arkansas chicken producers. Waco, Texas, won a settlement from 14 dairies for polluting the watershed.

A cesspool by any other name

Imagine living near a facility that houses hundreds or thousands of animals in confined spaces—operations run by huge corporations headquartered far away. Massive fans blow air out of the sheds where hundreds of hogs live in crowded pens. The waste from hog sheds is kept in huge multi-acre open-air cesspools—which the industry picturesquely calls "lagoons"—and some of it is sprayed untreated on nearby fields. Runoff kills fish in nearby streams and rivers. The air near these places is so bad that working or playing outside is intolerable and respiratory illnesses are aggravated. Your health and the health of your neighbors decline. Your property values go down—by $26 billion nationwide.

Or maybe you *should* drive a cow....

Near Western Washington University's campus in Bellingham, a team from the university's Vehicle Research Institute have built a hybrid car that runs partly on ... digested cow manure (biomethane). A small dairy of 667 cows provides the raw materials, which the researchers assert can generate the energy equivalent of 100,000 gallons of gasoline a year. Hmmm, there are 9 million dairy cows nationwide, multiply that times poop production per cow, divide that into energy extracted.... This could give new meaning to the term "gas up your car."

Antibiotics

Antibiotics are given to farm animals to prevent epidemics. Sounds reasonable—until you remember that bacteria can become resistant to antibiotics, making them useless. The FDA says that 70% of all infection-causing bacteria have become resistant to the top antibiotics. This is a serious matter, as people are dying from infections that could once have been be cured. Ironically, the practice is no longer even profitable, giving a return of only 10 cents per dollar spent. To ranchers they're tempting ("the meat equivalent of Miracle Gro") but scientists and medical authorities are concerned about possible epidemics.

- Over two thirds of antibiotics made in the United States goes to livestock.
- Salmonella is becoming resistant to antibiotics, spawning new superbugs that have begun to cause human fatalities. Agencies worldwide are clamping down on antibiotic use in agriculture.
- The loss of antibiotics' effectiveness due to factory farming costs $1.5 billion a year in public health.

The trouble with factory farms is that they are raising more than pigs. They are raising drug-resistant bugs as well.

—Scientists at the University of Illinois

Hormones

Growth hormones are routinely given to factory farmed cattle, so they'll grow faster and can be killed sooner, increasing profits. Some experts are concerned that exposure to these hormones in the food supply can harm human health; scientists are studying whether they are responsible for the fall in the age of puberty.

Land and biodiversity

Clearing land for cattle range and crops reduces vegetation, especially mature trees, which are needed to take up carbon dioxide. When cattle move in, other animals and plants suffer. Desert tortoises, cottonwood trees, and golden trout are just a few of the species impacted. Mountain lions, bobcats, foxes, and other predators are legally killed by ranchers. Sedimentation and erosion occur when cattle graze in and around streams, which are contaminated by droppings. Trampling causes erosion in creeks and slopes, ultimately harming floodplains.

Keystone critters

Prairie dogs, intelligent mammals that communicate in barks and chirps, live in large underground colonies, benefiting other species such as burrowing owls, hawks, eagles, foxes, and badgers. That makes them a keystone species, one that is especially important in its ecosystem Before the western plains were settled and converted to human use, millions of prairie dogs lived there. But 95% of them had been killed by 1900, shot and poisoned by people who wanted their land. Defenders of Wildlife (in partnership with other organizations) recently relocated several hundred prairie dogs to a protected area in eastern Wyoming. These little critters won't have to worry about losing their land to cattle ranches.

Your tax dollar

By the way, you are paying for all this. Besides cleaning up environmental damage that CAFOs cause, the federal government paid out over $245 billion dollars in farm subsidies (including non-meat farming) in the years 1995-2009.

- A rancher pays $1.35 a month per cow and calf to graze them on federal land. This is less than it costs to feed a house cat.
- Between 1995 and 2005, 74% of federal subsidies went to meat and dairy, and only 0.37% —that's one third of one percent—to fruits and vegetables.

Are cattle ranches all bad? A case has been made that well-managed ranches can exist in greater harmony with nature—if important changes are made. Smart pasture operations keep cattle on carefully managed rangeland where they eat the grass nature intended and don't need antibiotics or produce the amount of waste that factory farms do. Will enough ranchers make these changes?

Not too many, not too few–just right

Steve and Jane Sinton manage an 18,000-acre ranch. Instead of cramming as many cows as possible onto their land, Steve and Jane keep just as many cattle as the land can support, even during dry years. "You have to graze at the right level," he says. "Our philosophy is to leave enough grass so that if it doesn't rain until February, the herd can make it." Knowing the land's carrying capacity is age-old wisdom that Steve and Jane are honoring at their ranch.

Meat and human health

Eating high on the food chain exposes meat eaters to the chemicals given to the cows and chickens, and the toxins in the oceans the fish swam in. This is called bioaccumulation—risky substances increase the higher you go up the food chain. Furthermore, a diet heavy in animal protein (especially processed meat) increases risk of heart disease, infertility, and cancers of lung, breast, esophagus, and liver, while a vegetarian diet is associated with less obesity. In its official position paper, The American Dietetic Association says:

> The results of an evidence-based review showed that a vegetarian diet is associated with a lower risk of death from ischemic heart disease. Vegetarians also appear to have lower low-density lipoprotein cholesterol levels, lower blood pressure, and lower rates of hypertension and type 2 diabetes than nonvegetarians. Furthermore, vegetarians tend to have a lower body mass index and lower overall cancer rates.

Cardiologist Dean Ornish has shown that it is possible to reverse heart disease by a program of exercise, yoga, meditation—and a diet free of meat. Some elite athletes are vegetarians or vegans: marathoner Scott Jurek, pro baseball pitcher Pat Neshek and manager Tony LaRussa, tennis great Martina Navratilova, Iron Man champion Dave Scott, and many more. Omitting meat hasn't hurt their health—or their success.

> I don't understand why asking people to eat a well-balanced vegetarian diet is considered drastic, while it is medically conservative to cut people open and put them on powerful cholesterol-lowering drugs for the rest of their lives.
>
> —Dean Ornish, MD

And what's good for us is good for the planet. Experts David and Marcia Pimentel concluded, "The lacto-ovo-vegetarian diet [includes dairy and eggs] is more sustainable than the average American meat-based diet."

27

All of these facts—about grain conversion, water pollution, pesticides, biodiversity, and health—point to the same conclusion: The less meat we eat, the better off we are, and so is the planet.

What you can do:

✓ Eat less meat, or none. Have some meals with no meat, or one meatless day a week.

✓ Have smaller portions. Stretch meat in soups and stews, using spices to make them interesting.

✓ Go vegetarian. There are endless tasty dishes you can make without meat.

✓ If you eat meat, buy it from organically fed and more humanely raised animals. (See the chapter on Sustainable and More Humane Agriculture). Look for the new "100% grass fed" label. Visit americangrassfed.org.

✓ Visit the interactive map, factoryfarmmap.org, to track factory farms near you.

Prescription produce

Some Massachusetts doctors are taking active steps to help low-income children adopt a healthier diet. They're advising their patients to buy "prescription produce" at local farmers' markets–and even giving them coupons to help them pay for it. Since obesity costs this country $14 billion to treat health problems in children, and $147 billion in adults, this seems like a sensible preventive effort. In fact, 36 states have programs to encourage women and young children to benefit from the healthful produce available at farmers' markets. Luckily, in the U.S. there are over 6,000 farmers' markets (with total annual sales of over $1 billion), and more are opening all the time.

Dairy and Eggs

Dairy seems to be so healthy and innocuous, almost mythically innocent and nourishing. We find it in milk, cheese, ice cream, and dozens of other foods. But contrary to the well-funded advertisements, milk is not so healthy. Scientists have found that milk may increase risk of Parkinson's disease, breast and ovarian cancers, insulin resistance, and metabolic syndrome, which can lead to diabetes. How can the facts be so different from what we've always been taught? That image of cows' milk as "nature's perfect food" is promoted by ad campaigns paid for by the dairy industry.

For most people, dairy isn't a problem in reasonable quantities. However, some people, such as African Americans and Asians, have lactose intolerance—difficulty digesting dairy—more than Caucasians do. You do need calcium. It's available in many vegetables (such as broccoli and spinach) and in fruits (oranges, figs), nuts and seeds (almonds and sesame seeds), grains (quinoa and amaranth), tofu, and more.

Eggs may cause less environmental damage than beef, but if they come from chickens that live their lives in battery cages, they involve the same issues of cruelty, unsanitary conditions, grain conversion, and greenhouse gases that we have already learned about.

What you can do:
- ✓ Reduce the amount of dairy and eggs you consume.
- ✓ Try tofu, soymilk, and rice and almond beverages.
- ✓ Use less cheese in your cooking.
- ✓ If you use dairy and eggs, buy organic and certified humane products.

Fish

We may think there are literally oceans of fish, reproducing freely, as inexhaustible as the seas. Sadly, this is not true. We threaten fish (and crustaceans, mollusks, and marine mammals) by overfishing and polluting their water world. By the middle of this century, many edible species could be completely gone. The catastrophic oil gusher in the Gulf of Mexico in 2010 is only the latest event in our long record of damaging ocean life.

Overfishing

Humans have overfished throughout history, but modern methods take this to an extreme. Vast fleets of floating packing factories armed with sonar and advanced technologies are so efficient that they are engaged in "underwater clear-cutting." One hundred million tons of wild and farmed fish are sold annually. Fish being caught are getting smaller over time, as we kill off the larger ones.

- Fishing methods include metal chain dredges that uproot living organisms that attach to seafloors. Nets with rubber tires attached allow fishers to troll over rocky bottoms that were once inaccessible.
- The "mudtrails" left by trawlers dragging their equipment on the ocean bottom can be seen from space in satellite photos.
- 85% of species in the Mediterranean are overfished. Europe has so overfished its own waters that subsidized European fishing fleets are being sent to Africa.

Fish aren't the only ones to suffer. Jobs disappear when fisheries go out of business from overfishing; 40,000 jobs were lost when Canada's Atlantic cod fishery collapsed in the 1990s, and it has yet to recover. Over 72,000 jobs were lost in the Pacific Northwest due to declining stocks. In 2008 and 2009, the fishing season was closed on the West Coast.

There's some good news. In "catch share" programs, a percentage of a fishery's permitted catch is allotted to individuals or groups, who get a specified share of the coming season's catch. Members are free to buy and sell their shares to each other. This plan gives fishers a vested interest in making sure the entire area is well managed, rather than encouraging them to catch as many fish as possible. This approach has led to healthier fish populations, greater revenues for the fishers, and reduced bycatch.

Other solutions: Sea Change Investment Fund helps seafood distributors to do business in a more environmentally safe way. CleanFish is building a network of sustainable seafood producers. Stream restoration, often done by volunteer groups, helps salmon reach their home spawning grounds.

Bycatch and competition

Even species that are not wanted for food are at risk. Bycatch consists of the unwanted fish, crustaceans, and marine mammals that are caught in traps or nets, and thrown back into the sea dead or dying. For every pound of shrimp caught, seven pounds of other sea life are killed. In Japan, dolphins are herded into bays and slaughtered because they compete with humans for fish.

Science teacher Andrew Snow served as a biological observer for five years, living and working on Russian, Korean, and Japanese trawlers to enforce fishing regulations in the economic zone around the U.S. Each trawler put out a dragnet half a mile wide at the mouth and 100 yards wide at the narrow end, 3 to 5 times a day for 4 to 5 hours each time and dragged it across the ocean bottom, scraping off all life in its path. One ship could catch 500 tons of fish, but it also brought up crabs, shellfish, sea stars, and mammals. The crews left the unwanted animals to die on the deck or in the hold, and dumped them overboard before the catch was weighed.

Some boats would seek out breeding grounds, scooping up the fish that were trying to create the next generation, catching 300 to 400 tons of fish a day. Since freezer space was valuable, they kept only the eggs and threw the fish overboard. Corals were carelessly destroyed if they got in the way; five-foot high beautiful cone-shaped sponges were torn off, crushed, and thrown overboard. Snow estimates that a fleet of six trawlers threw out 100,000 tons of fish in one six-week season. He also saw American trawler workers shoot sea lions and killer whales that were attracted by nets full of fish.

Big businesses and the golden goose

Ecologist Paul Ehrlich was once told by a Japanese journalist that the Japanese whaling industry was knowingly exterminating the very source of its wealth. When Erhlich expressed surprise, the journalist said, "You are thinking of the whaling industry as an organization that is interested in maintaining whales; actually it is better viewed as a huge quantity of capital attempting to earn the highest possible return. If it can exterminate whales in ten years and make a 15% profit, but it could only make 10% with a sustainable harvest, then it will exterminate them in ten years. After that, the money will be moved to exterminating some other resource." Sad to say, the same could be said of many American businesses.

> Fishing in the ocean is no longer sustainable. Worldwide, we have failed to manage the ocean's fisheries—in a few decades, there may be no fisheries left to manage.
>
> —Fish expert John Marra

Dead zones and dams

Agricultural runoff (pesticides, antibiotics, fertilizer, and manure) enters the nation's creeks and flows downstream to lakes and oceans, killing marine life in more than a third of our coastal areas. Fish living in these toxins absorb pesticides, dioxins, PCBs, cadmium, and mercury, dangerous substances that end up in our food supply. Oceans are beginning to resemble open sewers.

When agricultural fertilizer reaches waterways, algae grow explosively; when the algae die, they sink to the bottom of the ocean or estuary and take up oxygen while they decompose. This creates oxygen-starved areas of water so depleted of oxygen by pesticide and industrial runoff that nothing can live there. Such dead zones exist around the world. The largest is located where the Mississippi River empties into the Gulf of Mexico; in 2007 it was 7,900 square miles (about the size of Connecticut and Delaware together). Dead zones are also hard on bottom-dwelling creatures such as crabs and oysters.

Dams pose another danger. To provide reservoirs and cheap hydroelectric energy, we have dammed many of the nation's rivers. Salmon in the Pacific Northwest find it almost impossible to reach their home streams to produce the next generation. Fortunately, some older dams are being taken down and natural waterways restored. The water of Manatawny Creek in Pennsylvania improved so much after a dam was removed in 2000 (and other stream restoration measures were taken) that the creek was taken off the state's impaired list.

Buying the dams

Hydroelectric dams block the Penobscot River in Maine, obstructing the spawning grounds of Atlantic salmon. Now the Penobscot River Restoration Trust (made up of environmental groups and native American tribes) is buying the dams from the power company. The trust will demolish the dams, the power company will be allowed to generate more electricity at its other dams, and a thousand miles of freshwater river and creeks will be restored, so fish can return. This abundance can support other native life such as river otters, bald eagles, and the Penobscot tribal culture.

Poisoned streams and oceans threaten our health

Other sources of water pollution are ship fuel and raw waste dumped into the water, and mercury released into the air when we burn fossil fuels. Every year, 60,000 babies are born in the United States with neurological problems caused by mercury—much of caused by the fish their mothers ate during pregnancy.

- California gold miners used millions of pounds of mercury in their hydraulic mining operations. Fish living in waters nearby still have dangerous mercury levels and have been declared unsafe for human consumption. What miners did 150 years ago is impacting us today.
- Some restaurants in New York are so concerned about mercury and the laxity of government inspections that they are testing fish themselves.

Compassion in action

Twenty-nine-year-old Achmat Hassiem was attacked by a shark while practicing for his lifeguard duties. Even though he lost his foot, he hopes to save sharks–from humans. While fewer than a dozen people a year die worldwide from shark attacks, 73 million sharks a year are killed for the main ingredient of just one dish, shark fin soup. After their fins are cut off, sharks are dumped back into the ocean to drown or bleed to death. This is unacceptable to many people–including Achmat and eight other survivors of shark attacks who are campaigning to save the animals. Australian navy diver Paul de Gelder, who lost his right hand and lower leg to a shark, says, "Regardless of what an animal does according to its basic instincts of survival, it has its place in our world."

Fish farming

Fish farming (aquaculture) would seem like the answer. But operators build large pens where they raise thousands of salmon, shrimp, or other fish, giving them antibiotics and possibly pesticides in their feed. Some, like salmon and shrimp, are carnivorous and are fed other fish which come from the oceans. One expert calculated that it takes two to three pounds of wild-caught fish to raise one pound of salmon or shrimp; another expert thinks the ratio is nearly five to one. This is net protein loss.

- Large tracts of the world's coastal forests and wetlands have been destroyed by coastal development or shrimp pond aquaculture.
- "Tuna ranches" catch young fish, fatten them, and slaughter them before they have a chance to reproduce—a recipe for extinction.

National laws and international treaties protect a few ocean species, such as whales and dolphins. But the treaties have been watered down, poorly enforced, or even repealed. Japan catches whales for scientific "research" of dubious value and sends their flesh to meat packing plants. Sanctuaries are not guarded or may actually permit fishing, boating, or mining.

Some progress is being made. More than 20 nations have agreed to restrict deep-water bottom trawling in response to a U.N. resolution. Walmart, which sells 50 million pounds of shrimp a year, is now requiring its shrimp suppliers in Thailand to be certified as sustainable. The Nature Conservancy has protected 3.8 million acres of sea floor by buying fishing permits from those who are willing to get out of the business, and converting their boats to research or patrol duty. The first sustainable tuna fishery has been certified by the Marine Stewardship Council. The California Fisheries Fund gives revolving loans to fishers to help them finance sustainable fishing practices. These steps make a start at preventing extinctions of food fish.

You can help by making wise food choices. But given the health benefits of fish we keep hearing about, is it really wise to give up fish?

First, remember that some fish are contaminated and not good for you at all. Second, if you're really concerned about your health, start by doing the other things doctors and nutritionists recommend (reduce saturated fats and heavily processed foods, eat more fresh fruits and vegetables, consume less meat), and get that exercise you're also supposed to do. These health choices don't cost lives.

What you can do:

✓ Eat less seafood, or none. Get omega-3 fatty acids in flax, walnuts, and canola oil.

✓ If you do eat seafood, choose the less endangered species and look for the Marine Stewardship Council certified label.

✓ Avoid Chilean sea bass, orange roughy, bluefin tuna, grouper, Atlantic cod, yellowfin tuna, flounder, monkfish, shark, shrimp, farmed salmon, American lobster, lingcod, rockfish, snapper, and rock cod.

✓ To reduce the perceived need for hydroelectric dams, use less electricity in all your activities: don't run the television for background noise, turn off lights and computers that are not in use, and air dry your laundry instead of using the dryer.

✓ Join coast and stream restoration activities, such as the annual Coastal Cleanup which takes place every September. People living inland can help the oceans by clearing their creeks of trash, which is otherwise carried downstream to oceans.

Fish facts are volatile, so keep up to date. See these web sites:

- Environmental Defense Fund, environmentaldefense.org
- Monterey Bay Aquarium, montereybayaquarium.org
- Marine Stewardship Council, msc.org
- Natural Resources Defense Council, nrdc.org/wildlife/fish

Who ya gonna call?
Blue Ocean Institute's FishPhone is a cell phone service that will instantly tell you if a fish is produced sustainably. At a store or restaurant, you text message FISH and the kind of fish you're considering to 30644. You'll get an instant reply rating it from red (avoid) to green (sustainable). Since 2007, the service has responded to almost 100,000 text messages.

More humanely raised meat, dairy, and eggs

Farmed animals are jammed into horribly confined pens, fed unnatural diets, and the ones that don't die first are slaughtered on fast-moving assembly lines that do not always stun them before they are knifed. No wonder this is called "factory farming."

There is an alternative to this cruelty. Humane Farm Animal Care, certifiedhumane.org, certifies growers as humane. The Humane Society persuaded Compass Group, the world's largest provider of food services, to switch to cage-free farming and helped persuade over 300 colleges and universities, as well as companies such as AOL and Google, to reduce or eliminate purchases of eggs from caged hens. You can help by buying humanely produced meat, dairy, and eggs.

However, the labels can be confusing and have been abused by industry. The term "cage-free" is given to companies that apply for it without being inspected. The phrase "has access to outdoors" may mean that in each huge building where thousands of chickens spend their lives, a small door is open to a small patch of pavement for one hour a day. "Free-roaming" means the chickens are not in cages, but they may still be jammed in a vast barn with thousands of other chickens with little or no access to outdoors. Some terms are completely meaningless—the word "natural" is not regulated.

What you can do:

- ✓ Eat less meat, or none.
- ✓ If you eat meat, choose meat from more humanely raised and slaughtered animals.
- ✓ Use eatwellguide.org to locate farms, restaurants, and stores near you that sell organic foods and more humanely raised meat.
- ✓ Patronize restaurants that serve meat from more humanely raised animals.
- ✓ Support legislation to protect farm animals.

Every hour in the United States, one million animals are killed for human consumption. If each one of us cuts back on our animal consumption by only 10%, approximately one billion animals would be spared a lifetime of suffering each year.

—The Humane Society of the United States

Soy

Soybeans are lower on the food chain and full of protein. They can be turned into a dazzling array of things, from soymilk to tofu, baked goods, veggie burgers, and more.

What you can do:

- ✓ Eat soybeans directly, cooking them like any other legume.
- ✓ Drink soymilk hot, serve it cold with cereals, and use it in recipes that call for milk.
- ✓ Use tofu as you would use eggs in baked goods, scrambles, casseroles, and more.
- ✓ Try tempeh (a fermented form of soy), miso (a bouillon-like concentrate), and frozen tofu desserts.

Veggie burgers

Veggie burgers, tofu burgers, and tempeh burgers are prepared patties. They come in many delicious flavors and are made of oats, grains, beans, and chopped vegetables; some include tofu or cheese. Many restaurants now offer veggie burgers, so you can continue to patronize your favorite establishments or accompany friends to theirs.

What you can do:

✓ Buy veggie burgers in your grocery or natural food store.

✓ Order veggie burgers at restaurants and encourage restaurants to stock them.

✓ Realize that there are many brands of veggie burger. If you don't like the first one you try, try another one.

✓ Learn a recipe for making your own veggie burgers. Many tasty combinations of oats, seeds, eggs, tofu, vegetables, rice, and nuts can easily be made with a blender and then baked or sauteed. Make large batches and freeze some for future meals.

Eat Shorter on the Food Chain

America's food marketplace is vast in dollars—and miles. In the United States, food travels an average of 1,500 miles to reach you. That is a very long food chain!

The global cornucopia and its cost to the Earth

Sometimes a lot of miles are racked up before the food even becomes food. Bees from Australia are flown to San Francisco and trucked to the Central Valley, where they are used to pollinate almond trees. The almonds are shipped to Spain for processing and then to Japan for baking. Meanwhile, fish caught in Norway's waters are frozen and shipped to China to have tiny bones removed by hand, then back to Norway for sale.

Such travel is possible because of increased transportation networks and cheaper labor abroad. But long convoluted supply chains can create problems—if foods are found to be tainted, who can tell where the contamination occurred? Experts admit, "Global supply chains have grown so long that some U.S. companies can't be sure where the products they're buying are made or grown."

Much of our food comes from monocultures orchestrated by big business. This means that a few corporate decision-makers can dictate how they crops they buy will be grown. By contrast, small farmers in your region can choose to keep their land healthier and their supply chains more transparent.

Smaller plots attract fewer pests than huge monoculture fields. There's less waste, because distances between field and customer are shorter and because knowledgeable consumers are willing to accept less-than-perfect-looking fruits and vegetables. Locally grown produce requires less gasoline and refrigeration to transport. And don't forget about another endangered species—farmers. Organic and sustainable agriculture are lifesavers for some of them. Small farmers who buck the trend toward industrialization and the pesticide tread-mill benefit from the popularity of organic foods, farmers' markets, and community supported agriculture.

As you might expect, greenhouse gases are involved. Shipping foods vast distances uses fuel and refrigerant chemicals. Another study found that eating a completely local diet would be like driving a car 1,000 fewer miles a year.

The Many Miles of a Fast Food Meal in Seattle

1. The cow is moved from a Texas range to a Colorado feedlot to be fattened.
2. Corn from Nebraska goes to the feedlot to feed the cow.
3. Water from the Ogalalla aquifer is used to water the cow.
4. The cow is slaughtered and the parts shipped to Seattle.
5. Milk from a dairy in Washington is turned into cheese.
6. Tomatoes and lettuce from California become garnish.
7. Wheat from Idaho becomes the hamburger bun.
8. Potatoes from Idaho become the fries.
9. Corn oil from Nebraska is used to fry the French fries.
10. Salt from Louisiana is added.
11. Florida tomatoes are shipped to Pittsburgh to make ketchup.
12. Ketchup is shipped to Ohio, where ketchup pouches are made.
13. Ketchup pouches are shipped from Ohio to Seattle.
14. The box for the fries is made of pulp from an Arkansas mill.
15. Bauxite from Australia is imported to make aluminum.
16. Calcium oxide from Japan is used to process the bauxite.
17. Aluminum goes from smelter to canner to make cans.
18. Corn from Iowa becomes the corn syrup to sweeten the cola.

Source: *Stuff: The Secret Life of Everyday Things* by John Ryan and Alan Durning (1997)

The adventure of the curious locavore

Can people truly shorten their food chains? Some adventurous souls tried it, inventing the "hundred-mile diet." The locavores' goal is to choose as many foods as they can that were grown within a hundred-mile radius of their homes. Locavores hold annual challenges, inviting people to try it for a month; you are allowed to name a few exceptions, if you absolutely must have coffee and imported spices. Think you'd have to live in the nation's breadbasket to make this work? Two pioneers, Alisa Smith and J.B. Mackinnon, did it for a year in Vancouver. Reflecting on all they'd learned about where and how food is grown, they concluded, "Distance is the enemy of awareness."

Eating locally is catching on. One market research firm believes that we will spend $7 billion on locally grown by 2011. College campuses are getting involved. For instance, the University of Vermont students asked for more local food, and within two months the food service shifted $50,000 of its purchases to local farmers.

Big and local

Bon Appetit is a café and cafeteria chain serving colleges, corporations, and museums. It is reducing its fuel consumption by buying more foods from within a 150-mile radius of the place where the food is served. That's a big impact, because Bon Appetit has over 400 restaurants in 29 states.

Obviously, in some parts of the country the hundred-mile diet would be more difficult than in others. And like most environmental issues, the food mile question is complicated. If a local farmer uses pesticides and drives the produce to market in a gas guzzler, the benefits of closeness are diminished. Critics suggest that the entire life cycle of the food should be taken into account; that meat eating is far more destructive; and that modes of producing food, not transporting it, create most of its greenhouse gas burden. And sure enough, some corporations are stretching the definition of "local" to cash in on the trend. Experts concluded that eliminating meat is even more powerful than eating locally. But since it offers many advantages beyond greenhouse gas reduction, I believe eating locally is part of a healthier food system.

Support your local farmer

In Community-Supported Agriculture (CSA) (also called subscription farming), small independent farmers plant a variety of crops. Subscribers pay an annual or monthly fee for a continuous succession of ripe goods. Fresh organic food is delivered to their homes or to specified pick-up locations. Some CSAs provide produce to local restaurants, roadside stands, or farmers' markets. There are over 2,500 subscription farms in the United States, in all 50 states.

Here's another creative idea. In Seattle, Pike Place Market Basket CSA is not a farm but a collective of 800 subscribers, which buys from over three dozen farms. This gives the subscribers all the advantages of a CSA while the farmers have a reduced burden of administration.

Community Supported Agriculture is one of the most exciting developments I've discovered. It gives farmers a chance to regain control of their livelihoods, the farms a chance to recover from pesticides, and purchasers a chance to participate in the healthy growing of Earth's bounty.

What you can do:

- ✓ Subscribe to a CSA farm. Find the ones nearest you at localharvest.org or checking out your local farmers' market.
- ✓ Ask about working shares in the farm, whereby you exchange several hours of work for a discount on your food.
- ✓ Apprenticeships and work exchanges let people experiment with the work of growing their own food.

What's green and grows in all 50 states?

The food-and-community program Farm to School connects schools with local farms. In Minnesota, 70 schools have joined the program. It does not require a large initial commitment—a school can start by just adding one item, such as local apples, to its offerings. That's how Dover-Eyota schools got started, and now it's adding other locally grown foods. Carrie Frank, nutrition director for the district, says, "This excites me–the opportunity to buy local, to buy the freshest. I've been in schools now for 17 years, and I don't know when I've been more excited to be in the industry. The students are quite proud of it. I hear comments like, 'My mom grew this.' Or one child said, 'My grandfather and I picked this.'"

Fresh food in season

Here's a radical experiment: Eat fresh foods only when they are in season. Instead of expecting fresh strawberries in January, do without until summer, or use frozen ones instead. This is a change from our homogeneous food world, where every month is the same as every other. Think of the holidays: would Christmas be so treasured if we celebrated it every week? Of course not. The long wait and the pleasure of anticipation are part of the fun. We enjoy birthdays, anniversaries, and graduations because they are not everyday events. Now just apply this appreciation to food. Look forward to the first ears of corn, the apples of late summer, the squash of autumn. Here's a glimpse of what you might expect:

- Early spring: Asparagus, root vegetables, dried beans
- Spring: Artichokes, fava beans, baby vegetables
- Late spring: Baby carrots, new potatoes, beets, snap peas
- Early summer: Berries, cherries, summer squash, plums
- Summer: Sweet corn, tomatoes, green beans, apricots
- Mid-summer: Herbs, eggplants, peppers, peaches, grapes
- Late summer: Early winter squash, sweet potatoes, okra

- Early autumn: Pumpkins, potatoes, apples, pears, figs
- Autumn: Chestnuts, winter squash, turnips, beets
- Winter: Cabbage, grapefruit, green onions, brussels sprouts
- Mid-winter: Root vegetables, lemons, limes, oranges
- Late winter: Root vegetables, winter greens, dried beans

The hundred-yard diet

You could even grow some food. What's more local than your own back yard? I have found great pleasure in growing apples, tomatoes, basil, squash, corn, and peaches, plus picking juicy wild blackberries and grinding wild acorns to make bread. In early spring, the blossoms signal the renewal of life. Soon you see little buds, and week by week you tend and admire the growing fruit. Finally, it's time to pick and enjoy your crop, the freshest, cleanest, and tastiest food you can imagine. Later in this book I'll tell you more about growing your own food.

You don't have to be a locavore purist to shorten your food chain. Just cut out the items that come the farthest and seek out foods grown by your local growers. You may be surprised how close they are. Some long-distance food may be hard to identify, especially if the ingredients in processed food were assembled at a manufacturing plant. Here are 7 easy ways to reduce your food miles.

What you can do:
✓ Eliminate the farthest food first. Wine from South Africa, apples from New Zealand—these are easy to identify and avoid. You still have the same foods; just choose ones grown nearer to you.
✓ Eat fresh foods only in season.
✓ Go just one time to a farmers' market. Spend a few dollars. I suspect you'll go back again.
✓ Join a CSA.
✓ Patronize restaurants that emphasize local ingredients.
✓ Shop at Whole Foods, which purchases from local suppliers.

45

✓ Host a potluck, asking guests to bring food grown locally. This is a memorable theme for a fall party, recalling the age-old celebration of Harvest Home.

Persuasive locavore

Kendra Okolita of Geneva, Illinois, mother of four children under age 6, inspired 902 of her friends and neighbors to pledge to eat more locally grown food. By recruiting so many new locavores, Kendra won a contest run by New American Dream, an organization that helps citizens become responsible consumers. Her prize? A landscaping makeover.

Eat Wider on the Food Chain

The Earth provides an astounding variety of edible life forms. Do you know what a daikon is? (A delicious mild radish). Have you ever heard of feijoa? (A fruit, also called pineapple guava). Not so long ago, kiwis were unknown in America, and now they are familiar fruits. Many other foods are just waiting to reach your table.

Yet we're putting all our eggs in a few genetic baskets. Three quarters of the world's calories consumed by humans come from seven crops (wheat, rice, corn, potato, barley, cassava, and sorghum). The genetic diversity of even these few crops is rapidly disappearing, as their native habitats are being destroyed and fewer varieties of each species are being cultivated. We need to make our food chain wider by choosing more diversity.

But isn't there is a contradiction between the "eat local" guideline and the "choose diversity" guideline? Only if you interpret "choose diversity" to mean buying the most exotic foods that traveled the longest distance to reach you. Actually, you can honor both guidelines. First, let's look at the problem of food diversity.

Diversity in danger

Loss of diversity can be a problem. Modern corn, which is used in almost 200 food products, clothing, drugs, and even cosmetics, was decimated by a fungus in 1970. Fortunately, there were still some wild varieties in existence; genetic material from the wild helped breed resistance to the fungus into the corn crop. What if there hadn't been any wild ones left?

> Seeds are the software of the natural world that has taken millions of years to develop, and we don't know how we will need them in the future.
>
> —Roy Steiner of the Gates Foundation,
> which funds The Global Crop Diversity Trust

Eccentrics to the rescue

Fortunately, heirloom seeds are being saved and shared by dedicated individuals and groups that have rescued many varieties, keeping genetic material alive. Chefs Collaborative, Slow Food, American Livestock Breeds Conservancy, the Global Crop Diversity Trust, and the U.N. International Treaty on Plant Genetic Resources are racing to save species from extinction.

Some precious varieties are kept only by a few aged individuals. If these people die without handing over their seeds and the knowledge to grow them, the species can die out. In Italy, one plant scientist found that a third of the crops she once found being grown by Tuscan households had already been abandoned–in less than a decade.

The wine detective

Where are the missing grapevines? Marco Reinotti is on the case. In the northern Italian wine region Val d'Aosta, he searches for neglected grape varieties on the verge of extinction. One variety, Vuillermin, was known only from nineteenth-century books and pictures until a few vines were rediscovered in 1989. Reinotti continues his gumshoe work tracking down other almost-lost wine grape varieties.

The solution

Remember that apparent contradiction between local and diversity? You can help strengthen our food diversity, without burdening the earth with long-distance shipping, by making three kinds of food choice: broadening your selections of foods that are grown in the U.S., choosing unusual varieties of common foods, and choosing grains and produce that originated far away but that are now grown here.

Diversity in fruits, vegetables, and grains

You can buy unusual varieties of familiar foods such as apples and potatoes, buy unusual foods, or even grow some in your garden. The names alone are worth the price.

- Apples: Pink Ladies, Cameos, Criterions, Jonagolds, and other varieties.
- Potato varieties: Yukon Gold, Kennebec, Norchip, Norkotah, Shepody, and Sebago.
- Tomatoes: Sun Gold, Brandywine, Stupice, Black Prince, Green Zebra, Earl of Edgecombe, and Costoluto Genovese, Cherokee Purple, Mortgage Lifter, Hawaiian Pineapple, Eva Purple Ball, Arkansas Traveler, and Box Car Willie.

It's also becoming easier to find exotic foods: carambola, cherimoya, atemoya, guava, purple passionfruit, persimmon, and tamarillo. Have you ever tried the moon-and-stars watermelon or the tepary bean or Ojai pixie tangerines? Grains exist in a delicious assortment, too. New varieties of rice and wheat have arrived on our shelves, and grains like amaranth, spelt, and quinoa (pronounced keen-wa) are finding a place in American cuisine.

The potato rainbow

At 13,000 feet above sea level in the Peruvian Andes, villagers harvest potatoes of an amazing rainbow of colors (red, yellow, purple, pink with yellow spots) and shapes (round, oblong, twisted, spiral). The amazingly versatile potato is the fourth most important food crop in the world, but its genetic diversity is being endangered by habitat loss and monoculture. The International Potato Center (CIP), based near Lima, is one of the world's 1,500 gene banks for food. Its mission is to preserve the genetic diversity of potatoes. By making seeds available through its website, CIP is a Noah's ark of tubers, passing down the rainbow of potatoes to future generations.

Diversity in protein

According to the UN's Food and Agriculture Organization, 20% of the world's livestock breeds are in danger. One livestock breed goes extinct every month. Beef, pork, fish, eggs, and chicken are primary sources of Americans' animal protein, but we have narrowed our output to a few varieties. Some individuals and organizations are working to revive breeds that have almost died out. Ethnic cuisines are rich in diversity, such as eggs from quail and ducks, unusual fish, and organ meats. In some cultures, it's common to eat insects—fried ants in Mexico, termite and palm grubs in Colombia, grasshoppers and crickets in the Philippines. That's really eating low on the food chain!

Many sources of protein do not require animals at all. Legumes (peas and beans) exist in a pleasing variety and can be made into soups, appetizers, and main courses. The soybean is a protein champion; in the form of tofu, it can serve as a versatile alternative to eggs in every kind of recipe—cakes, casseroles, burgers, and more—and made into non-dairy beverages and frozen desserts.

Diversity in sweeteners

Refined cane sugar, corn syrup, and artificial sweeteners form a huge part of the modern diet. The average American consumes 20 teaspoons of added sugars a day, accounting for 16% of our calories. High-fructose corn syrup—a highly processed substance that manufacturers have been allowed to call "natural"—is put into sodas, ketchup, soup, and baked goods. So what could you use instead? Other delicious alternatives available at health food stores are barley malt, molasses, fruit concentrate, and beet sugar. Stevia is an enticing prospect. It comes from a plant native to Paraguay that is now being grown in many regions. Stevia is 250 times sweeter than sugar, which means you use so little you get almost no calories. Find it in powdered form at Whole Foods or health food stores.

The fat of the land?

Obesity in the U.S. is rising. (If anyone tells you it's all genetic, ask them why the obesity rate has skyrocketed within one generation). In 2009, not a single state has an obesity rate lower than 15%. That means at least one person in seven is not just pudgy, not just overweight, but seriously, dangerously fat. Obesity has many causes, but WHAT you eat, not just how much, is key. Eating less processed food and more fresh fruits and vegetables can help. Luckily, the earth has given us a spectacular variety of foods to choose from. Even your regular grocery store probably has more food diversity than you've realized. In the produce aisles, look at the higher shelves or corners that you ordinarily walk past. Jerusalem artichokes, jicama, tomatillos, Braeburn apples.... Finding, preparing, and enjoying these will give both health and pleasure.

How to do diversity

Try one new food a week. You could try a new protein source one week, a new fruit the next week, a new vegetable the third week. You'll love some of them, reserve judgment on some, and not like some—that's what experimenting is all about. Shop in a part of town you don't usually visit. You might find banana blossoms, durian, lotus roots, wal quay sum, gai lan, gai choy, gobo, nagaimo, and seaweed from Chinese markets. From Mexico we get red corn, tomatillos, and nopales (cactus). The Hmong people from Southeast Asia eat lemongrass, red basil, bitter eggplant, and lotus roots. Your region may have other intriguing ethnic cuisines. Interview older members of your family, who may remember foods from just a generation or two ago.

Where to find unusual foods:

- Ethnic aisles of your regular supermarket
- Your supermarket's produce department. (Look on shelves you tend to ignore)
- Natural grocery stores such as Whole Foods
- Farmers' markets
- Community Supported Agriculture
- Ethnic food stores and restaurants

How to prepare unusual foods:

✓ Search the web for recipes and food information.

✓ Explore the cookbook section of your local bookstore.

✓ Investigate cooking classes in your community.

✓ Some fresh produce is sold with stickers that give brief instructions.

✓ Some grocery stores and CSAs farms give recipes for unusual foods.

Noah's Archives

A modern Noah's Ark has been built in a cave under a remote mountain in Norway, where scientists have stored seeds of thousands of varieties of plants. There, the Global Crop Diversity Trust is protecting "orphan crops" as well as the established ones. This "ultimate safety net" will give the world a kind of genetic insurance. This is good news, but it's sad that we've so depleted nature that we have to put its seeds under lock and key.

Nude Food

Soon after Andy Keller was laid off from his software job, he ran an errand at his local dump and was shocked at what he saw. "There were plastic bags everywhere, with birds pecking at them, or caught on the fences," he said. "I made a commitment to myself to adopt a healthier reusable bag habit. And then I thought, 'I can make a business out of this.'" So he did. His company, ChicoBag, makes light nylon grocery bags that can be packed into their own attached pouch, so it's easy to keep one with you. Keller was right about the waste. We've all heard that question at the checkout counter: "Paper or plastic?" Answer: Neither. A reusable cloth or nylon bag is better by far.

Less packaging

Canadian activists at Environnement Jeunesse think food should be "Naked, Near, Natural, and Just." That is, minimally packaged (naked), local (near), grown with few or no chemicals (natural), and from farmers who get a fair wage (just). But our food is overdressed. Millions of tons of resources go into packaging—trees cut down for paper, petroleum turned into plastic, minerals dug up to make aluminum and steel, plus energy and oil required to run the factories that make the packaging. It also takes energy and packaging to get ingredients from one processing plant to another. Did you know we use 215 billion beverage containers a year, 30 billion of them single-serving plastic drink bottles?

Unfortunately, much of this packaging is not recycled or land-filled, but released into the environment. Even the oceans have become our dumping grounds. The Great Pacific Garbage Patch is a swath of the ocean between California and Hawaii where millions of tons of our discards have been deposited by ocean currents and broken down into small particles. The result has been called "plastic soup" and "floating landfill."

Some plastic is actually dangerous. Bisphenol A (BPA) is an estrogen-like compound used to make hard plastic containers. More than

53

6 million pounds of BPA are produced in the U.S. each year and used in CDs, DVDs, eyeglasses, dental sealants, the liners of food cans, plastic water bottles, and major brands of infant formula. BPA, a hormone disruptor, leaches into the bottle's contents and contributes to reproductive harm to humans, as well as heart disease and diabetes.

We are doing better at recycling and reusing these valuable materials, but there is waste involved in transporting them back to a factory and remanufacturing them. So let's cut to the chase—buy stuff with less packaging to begin with.

What you can do:
- ✓ Buy products with the least packaging: Fresh, local, in season. Be willing to buy produce that is perfectly good, though it might not look perfect.
- ✓ Buy products in bulk or large containers, not tiny serving sizes.
- ✓ Use concentrates (juices, cleansers), which require less packaging.
- ✓ When buying a few small items, ask the clerk not to put them in a bag.
- ✓ Reuse and recycle the packaging you can't avoid.
- ✓ Bring your own cloth bags. Many grocery and drug chains sell them, as do online retailers. Some stores give you a small rebate for bringing your own bags.
- ✓ Eat your packaging. Buy ice cream in cones, not plastic cups.

A little quiz
- Q. If most of the California wine shipped to the eastern U.S. were sent in wine boxes instead of bottles, how much greenhouse gas would be eliminated? **A:** 2 million tons.
- Q. How many cars would have to be taken off the road to equal that saving? **A:** 400,000.

Less processing

Processing is the work of cooking and assembling the food; adding coloring, additives, and preservatives; putting it into boxes, bottles, or cans; and shipping it from one plant to another, each time using gasoline and packaging and diminishing the product's natural nutrients. Add the environmental cost of building the machines (steel, plastic, etc.) and the pollution generated to run them.

Agribusiness sends most of its crops for processing—it's more profitable than fresh. A typical cleaning and grading procedure may include the following steps:

- Offloading belt. Harvested beans go from the truck to a belt conveyor.
- Gravity separator. Adhering soil, rocks, and heavy field trash drop out.
- Trash eliminator. An air blast removes leaves, stems, and other trash.
- Pin-bean eliminator. A rotating drum removes immature pods.
- Broken-bean eliminator. A rotating tumbler removes broken pods.
- Vibrating tables. Good pods are further segregated from field trash.
- Vibrating washers. Pods are rinsed with clean water.
- Grading tables. Pods are inspected to remove defective ones.
- Carousel-type automatic box filler. Beans are moved into boxes.
- Automatic box-closing machine Boxes are closed.
- Cooling. Filled containers are cooled, and stored or shipped.

French fries in fast food restaurants are probably Russet Burbanks—90% of Idaho's potatoes are of this variety because fast food chains prefer it. To grow each potato, 7 ½ gallons of water are used, water diverted from rivers, depriving fish of their habitat.

Fertilizers and pesticides are used to grow the potato, contaminating waterways with the runoff. The potato is harvested by a diesel machine and trucked to a processing plant. Freezing the potatoes requires electrical energy, encouraging the building of more hydro-electric dams, and uses hydrofluorocarbon coolants in a refrigerated 18-wheeler diesel truck.

When the potatoes reach the factory, after conveyor belt sorting they are steamed, shot through a water gun knife, and emerge as potato slices. Video cameras pick out imperfect ones, which are sent to machines that cut out flaws and return them to the line. The potatoes then move through more hot water, air, and oil to become fries. Air cooled by ammonia gas freezes them, and more machines sort, seal, and load them for shipping. Finally, the fries are served in a cardboard carton, often with a handful of plastic ketchup packets, many of which are discarded unopened.

Ingredients of highly processed food move around from state to state, processing plant to processing plant to packaging plant, in what journalist Michael Pollan calls "an elaborate and energy-intensive choreography of ingredients." Cornell researchers, who discovered we could cut the fuel we use to produce food by nearly 50%, recommend that we eat less processed food. Junk the junk food and save the planet.

What you can do:
✓ Buy more fresh and locally grown produce.
✓ Buy products with the least processing and packaging.
✓ Grow some of your food.

Less waste

There is no waste in nature. Every plant, animal, rock, and drop of water is broken down and reused. Fallen trees, leaves, the shells left by a nut-eating squirrel, and the fur or feathers left by a predator are recycled in the ecosystem, decaying and becoming soil in which new plants and animals can live and grow.

We humans have disturbed this cycle, taking unwanted material to landfills, where it is junked with old batteries, turpentine, plastic containers, and other unnatural trash to be sealed off for decades. Waste occurs at the farm, the factory, the store, and the kitchen. Thirty percent of food, worth $48 billion, is thrown away every year just by households. Wasting food also means wasting water. One hamburger, for instance, takes over 600 gallons of water to produce. Food sent to the landfill also generates methane, a greenhouse gas much more damaging than carbon dioxide.

Let's learn from nature and eliminate the whole concept of waste. Some companies have already spotted the opportunity. In New Jersey, a new plant (creating local jobs) will put food waste into huge digester tanks with oxygen, microbes, and heat, to turn it into compost and fertilizer.

What you can do:
✓ Serve yourself only as much as you're likely to eat.
✓ Save and use leftovers.
✓ Compost the rest.

Waste? Not a concept

Biochar involves roasting organic material that would otherwise go to landfill, turning it into a powerful soil amendment. Scientists have found that native peoples in the Amazon region used biochar for thousands of years. One company, Biocharm, gets wood chips donated by arborists (who thereby save themselves the landfill fee), uses solar energy to dry the wood, then uses "waste heat" procured from sanitary and landfill operations (heat which would otherwise be lost) to complete the charring process. Biochar is thus more local than the garden fertilizers made from petroleum imported from overseas. Trip Allen of Biocharm told me that biochar solves three problems: it captures carbon to slow global warming, diverts materials from landfills (while also reducing truck fuel used to make those landfill dump runs), and improves topsoil. This sounds like win-win-win to me.

Glamour water and its sins

Who could have ever dreamed we would package *water*? In fact, it is a multi-billion-dollar-a-year industry in the U.S. In 2007, Americans consumed 8.8 billion gallons of it, even though some bottled water is nothing but tap water. One restaurant was going through 25,000 bottles of water a year.

- We use 5 billion plastic bottles a year and recycle only 25% of them. Water bottles have an even worse record: 86% of them become litter or garbage.
- It takes 1.5 million barrels of oil just to make the plastic water bottles for Americans, producing 2.5 million tons of carbon dioxide.

To fill its bottles, a corporation may tap water sources that local people depend on, and then ship the water hundreds or thousands of miles away. One company imports water from Fiji, the tropical islands halfway around the world, boasting that the water is pristine, sourced far from the touch of civilization. Behind this enticing illusion is the reality: shipping that burns gasoline and packaging that wastes plastic. Adding insult to injury, bottled water is not always purer than tap water, and in some cases less pure.

The rationale for buying bottled water is a fantasy that has a destructive downside. These companies are marketing an illusion of environmental purity.

—Dr. Gina Solomon,
National Resources Defense Council

But the party's over. The environmental costs of bottled water have made headlines. Communities are taking action. San Francisco decided in 2007 to ban bottled water in city offices after a newspaper revealed that it was spending $500,000 a year on the stuff. Some restaurants forego bottled water, even though they could make a big profit on it. To protect their local supplies, some states have declared groundwater a commonly owned resource that deserves protection.

What you can do:
✓ Don't buy glamour water. The appeal is mostly image.
✓ Reuse glass jars or get one of the new metal bottles made without Bisphenol A.
✓ When at theatres, convention centers, hospitals, and parks, find and use water fountains.

PART
II

PART II
Creating Your Green Foodprint

Every day it gets easier to find Earth-friendly foods. They're in supermarket chains, health food stores, farmers' markets, and subscription farms. In your local supermarket you'll find organic food in the produce section, meatless options in the frozen meal freezers, new products such as soy-based entrees or low-fat items, and diverse products such as Japanese eggplant and amaranth.

You can also help by patronizing green restaurants, eating Earth-friendly choices in other restaurants, and using solutions that already exist for catering, picnicking, camping, and at work—in fact, wherever you are.

Green is the new red, white, and blue.

—Thomas L. Friedman,
The New York Times

Making Your Foodprint Choices

If you're already making some green food choices, congratulations! If you're just entering the new food world, welcome. Here are some ideas for beginning (or improving) your green foodprint.

Start with your passion.

You may feel strongly about one issue (such as waste) and become inspired to take actions that reduce waste even more. Or, as you learn more about the new food world, you may want to explore different ways of greening your foodprint. Let your enthusiasm guide you. There's no one right path.

Small steps count.

With my psychologist hat on, I promise you that it's usually more effective—and more fun—to make a series of small steps successfully than it is to set an unrealistic goal that makes you feel anxious or guilty. You'll have thousands of opportunities every year to help save the Earth with your food choices.

Reward yourself.

Do this early and often. Praise yourself for making sustainable food choices, share your progress with a friend, put it on your blog, or indulge in a small or big treat (which might be a special food, or time to read your favorite book, or a visit with a friend).

Find Earth-friendly food.

The rest of this section of the book shows you where to find Earth-friendly food. It's easier than you might think!

Steps I can take:

1.

2.

3.

Grocery Stores

Major chains

Mainstream grocers are beginning to stock environmentally friendly foods. For instance, Safeway, with 1,775 stores in the U.S. and Canada plus almost 500 subsidiary stores, has created a house organic label for over 300 products, from fresh lettuce to spaghetti sauce. Safeway also won an award from California's Integrated Waste Management Board for its success in recycling and composting.

Health food chains

Whole Foods has 335 stores in North America and the United Kingdom, selling healthy organic food and personal care products. It scores high with Greenpeace on sustainable fish and makes low-interest loans in 12 states to small businesses that produce food crops, body care products, and artisan foods such as nut butters, ice cream, granolas and cheese. The company uses biodiesel in some of its distribution centers, composts food waste, uses green construction methods, recycles plastics, glass and aluminum at its stores, sells reusable shopping bags, offers a refund to shoppers who bring their own bags, and puts some prepared foods in compostable packaging. In 2010, it was recognized by the EPA as a Green Power Partner of the Year–for the third year in a row.

Upscale chains

Trader Joe's, My Organic Market, Harris Teeter, Publix, and Andronico's are some of the regional chains that sell Earth-friendly foods to a large and appreciative customer base.

The really green grocer

My Organic Market in the Washington DC area does a lot for the Earth. The stores use wind power, putting owner Scott Nash in the top 10 of EPA's green power retailers. They have a full-time environmental coordinator. Seafood is sustainably procured. Nash offers employees free compost bins, motion sensor lights, programmable thermostats, energy-efficient light bulbs, and financial incentives to buy energy-efficient appliances and cars and to have home energy audits. All this is not hurting business. Employee turnover has gone down, 95% reporting they are satisfied or happy at work, and Nash is opening new stores nearby.

Independent stores

Your local independent stores also have choices in the products they stock and the way they do business. Your area might also have independent natural food stores. You can shorten your food chain by buying locally grown food.

What you can do:

- ✓ Take a few extra minutes to look closely at the grocery shelves to see if your store is stocking organic, local, and Earth-friendly foods. Look on higher and lower shelves than you usually do and inspect aisles you usually skip.
- ✓ To avoid waste, ask yourself, "Will I really use this? When and how?"
- ✓ Take your own cloth bags, or re-use paper or plastic bags.
- ✓ Buy in bulk to reduce packaging.

Farmers' Markets and Roadside Stands

Farmers' markets

These are outdoor markets set up at specified hours in local malls or other public places, where the people who grow your food arrive in their own trucks and set up stalls. (Some market stands may be operated by small-scale middlemen). Purchasing fresh produce directly from growers is a pleasant change from supermarket shopping and allows you to support small local farms. According to the USDA, over 6,000 farmers' markets operate in the United States. Many of the stands offer organic produce. You can also meet your neighbors and even, at some markets, listen to live music and buy delicious cooked meals. Markets I've visited certify that the stands labeled organic really are organic.

Roadside stands

Roadside stands, where growers sell their fruits and vegetables in shops or sheds near their farms, can be found in rural regions, some of them not far from populated areas. You'll see handmade signs proclaiming Almonds or Berries or Apples as you drive along the road. These stands are typically seasonal, open during harvest time. Sometimes at the height of the harvest season, farmers will even announce Pick-Your-Own events, where you participate in harvesting your food.

What you can do:
- ✓ Locate the farmers' markets near you at these web sites: local harvest.org and ams.usda.gov/AMSv1.0/farmersmarkets
- ✓ Next time you see a roadside stand, or a sign pointing to one, check it out.
- ✓ Buy lots of fresh fruits and vegetables, then freeze or can some.

Restaurants

Americans are a mobile people. We relocate, we travel, we dine out a lot. Collectively, we spend almost half our food dollars and consume about half our daily calories away from home, at fast-food establishments, sit-down restaurants, in our cars, outdoors, at work, at play, and while traveling.

Sit-down restaurants

Restaurant portions are getting larger. What to do? Eating everything on the plate can contribute to overweight. Taking home leftovers prevents food waste, but creates packaging waste since leftovers are wrapped in foil or put into styrofoam or a paper bag–sometimes several of these at once.

What you can do:

✓ Order only what you can eat.
✓ Ask the server to omit things you won't eat (pickles, sour cream, potato chips).
✓ Share a main course if you're not very hungry.
✓ Order one course at a time; stop when you're full.
✓ Take home leftovers (only if not over-packaged).
✓ Tell the waiter (and manager and owner) why you chose the restaurant and why you're choosing your Earth-friendly entrée.

Fast food

Americans spent over $100 billion on fast food every year—more than we spent on higher education, personal computers, software, or new cars. It is more than we spent on books, movies, magazines, newspapers, videos, and recorded music combined. But fast food restaurants have not been doing well by the Earth. Large chains encourage monoculture, cruel factory farming of animals, intense food processing, and long-distance distribution.

What you can do:

- ✓ Order only what you can eat.
- ✓ Take only the condiments (ketchup, etc.) that you'll use.
- ✓ Don't take or accept more napkins than you need.
- ✓ Avoid the drive-through windows, especially if there is a long line of cars ahead of you. This is sedentary and wastes gas.
- ✓ Encourage the establishment to start serving veggie burgers. Then order them.
- ✓ Be aware of which fast food chains are beginning to take action to reduce their environmental impact.

Best of all: Support green restaurants

Green restaurants do some or all of the following:

- Serve a diverse selection of foods
- Offer vegetarian or vegan options
- Support the Chefs Collaborative commitment to serve only sustainable fish
- Purchase local ingredients from local organic growers
- Offer varying portion sizes to discourage overeating
- Compost
- Recycle
- Have a children's menu—small portions for small people
- Derive their energy from renewable sources
- Use energy efficiently.

And they use creativity. One Brooklyn restaurant runs its blender on bicycle power. Another sends coffee sacks to a local farmer for creative reuse over the winter; in the next harvest season, the farmer returns the bags to the restaurant full of vegetables.

Chefs Collaborative is a network of chefs, restaurateurs, and other food professionals promoting sustainable agriculture, supporting local farms, and educating us about clean, healthy food. Chefs Collaborative has chapters nationwide and offers information on the internet on which seafood species are endangered and should not be served.

> Food is fundamental to life, nourishing us in body and soul. The preparation of food strengthens our connection to nature. And the sharing of food immeasurably enriches our sense of community. Good food begins with unpolluted air, land, and water, environmentally sustainable farming and fishing, and humane animal husbandry. Food choices that emphasize delicious, locally grown, seasonally fresh, and whole or minimally processed ingredients are good for us, for local farming communities, and for the planet. Cultural and biological diversity are essential for the health of the Earth and its inhabitants. Preserving and revitalizing sustainable food, fishing, and agricultural traditions strengthen that diversity.
> —From Chefs Collaborative Statement of Principles

There may be green restaurants in your area. If not, you can help develop them by communicating with waiters and owners whenever you dine. Introduce them to the Chefs Collaborative. Show them your pocket card (available at montereybayaquarium. org) listing fish that are sustainable and those that are not.

For some people, driving across town or to the middle of nowhere is part of the dining event. Unfortunately, doing so pours gasoline emissions into the air. Consider patronizing establishments closer to home, carpooling to that great restaurant, or saving it for special occasions.

What you can do:

- ✓ Patronize green restaurants. Vegetarian restaurants and those near colleges and universities may be especially Earth-conscious.
- ✓ Encourage other restaurants to become green.
- ✓ Patronize local restaurants.
- ✓ Choose locally grown foods.
- ✓ Give a letter of appreciation to the restaurant manager or owner.

Early adopter

In Washington DC, environmentalists and politicians can rub shoulders at Restaurant Nora, which was the first restaurant in America to be certified organic. This means that at least 95% of the food was produced by certified organic growers. Among the tasty ingredients in her cuisine, Nora serves grass-fed beef, free-range chicken, hand-made cheese, heirloom tomatoes, and wild mushrooms—in season, of course.

Caterers

You or your workplace might hold a catered event—an office party, wedding, anniversary, or fund-raiser. If you arrange events frequently or if you're a food or hospitality professional, you could become especially knowledgeable about the green caterers in your area, or educate them to become green. Many caterers are small local businesses. You can influence them because, in hiring them, you are the boss. Ask the caterer to supply food that is organic, diverse, local, and prepared efficiently. Ask for little or no meat; if there is meat, it's farmed free or organic; and no endangered species.

Green caterers also:
- Share unserved food with food banks if local laws allow,
- Compost the scraps,
- Use reusable or compostable utensils,
- Use paper goods made from recycled paper, and
- Clean up using kinder cleansers, unbleached paper, and recycling.

Your role is to help estimate the amount of food needed. This will depend on the nature of the event (wedding or baseball tournament? Buffet or sit-down dinner?), the number of guests likely to attend, what time of day (mealtime or after school?), the age and activity level of the guests (seniors or teenagers?), and other factors that a knowledgeable caterer will encourage you to consider. You don't want to run out of food, and it's unlikely that you'll order the precise amount the entire party consumes; therefore, you'll probably have a surplus. Consider this when you plan your menu. Arrange for extras to be taken home, saved for the next day, or donated to food banks.

If you are the organizer of a club's or charity's regular events (fund-raising benefits, annual sporting tournaments), keep records on how much and what kind of food the people in your group tend to eat. You can also buy computer software to help you estimate quantities and select recipes based on preferred ingredients. The caterer will also help you estimate.

What you can do:

✓ Carefully estimate the amount of food you need. To avoid falling short, ask the caterer to have a backup item in reserve. You pay for this item; if it is not served, you can take it home.

✓ Renting china and tableware has less environmental impact than using disposable plates and utensils. If you choose the latter, make sure they're biodegradable.

✓ Arrange the timing of food preparation so that less is wasted.

✓ Coordinate with the caterer to control the temperature of preparing and holding food.

Earth-friendly ever after

The wedding industry is huge: $58 billion a year, plus $80 billion of indirect expenses. That's $25,000 per wedding—$600 just for the cake. The average wedding and honeymoon create 9 to 16 tons of CO_2 emissions. This big business of happiness, food, clothes, travel, and gifts is going green. More couples are starting their new lives together by celebrating their marriage in an Earth-friendly way. Forgoing diamond rings, throwaway cameras, and multi-paged invitations, couples are choosing wedding gowns made of organic silk or hemp and using organically grown flowers. In lieu of gifts, some ask loved ones to make donations to environmental causes. They ask caterers to think green, offering vegetarian options, organic and locally grown food, and managing the leftovers. Herban Feast Catering in Seattle goes even further, using biodegradable garbage liners, recycling, giving leftovers to shelters, and composting waste.

Picnicking, Camping, and the Back Yard Barbecue

Sometimes "away from home" means really away—camping in the woods. Yet we make a mess of the very places we travel so far to admire, leaving behind bottles, papers, and other trash. We throw food away rather than carry it home, accustoming wild animals to finding food in waste bins or thrown on the ground. This is not safe for them or for us. We may also buy highly processed and packaged convenience foods to take on our "nature" hikes. Remember the outdoor-lovers' motto: Take nothing but pictures and memories; leave nothing but footprints.

What you can do:
✓ Bring reusable utensils and then take them away with you.
✓ If you do use disposable plates, utensils, and cups, use ones made from cornstarch or other biodegradable materials. Then take them home and compost them.
✓ Put leftovers in reusable containers and take them home to eat later.
✓ Recycle everything recyclable.
✓ Properly dispose of all litter.
✓ To be a true eco-hero, you could clean up the litter left behind by others.

The back yard barbecue

Ah, back to nature. Cooking and eating outdoors like our ancestors…. But this rustic scene is not so innocuous. Each July 4, millions of people light their barbecue grills, burning the equivalent of 2,300 acres of forest, emitting nearly 225,000 metric tons of carbon dioxide. Particulates fill the air. Grease burns onto the grills and harsh cleansers are used to clean them. We can do better than this.

What you can do:

- ✓ Don't use lighter fluid to start the barbecue—it contributes to smog. Use a chimney starter instead, a metal cylinder with a handle into which you put your charcoal briquettes. They heat up much faster and require no lighter fluid.
- ✓ If you use charcoal briquettes, douse them with water after you're done cooking. This helps prevent fires and briquette pieces make good fixings to start the next fire.
- ✓ Corn on the cob can be grilled in its husk if you first soak it in water. This eliminates the need for aluminum foil.
- ✓ Replace meat with tasty vegetable skewers.
- ✓ Clean your grill promptly, using warm water and baking soda, before the burned food hardens and you are tempted to use harsh chemical cleaners.

Gourmet dirt

San Francisco collects food waste from all homes and also from 3,000 food-related businesses. This civic composting program has been so popular—collecting over 420 tons of food scraps and yard trimmings every day—that the waste companies had to add new facilities to handle it all. The resulting compost is sent to nearby vineyards, small farms, and landscape supply yards. Says Robert Haley of the city's Department of the Environment, "We combined innovative approaches, education, the mandate, and financial incentives to make this program such a success."

At Work, at Play, and on the Road

We spend a lot of time working, commuting, attending entertainments, driving ourselves and our kids to school and activities, and traveling. In all of these, there are opportunities to make Earth-friendly food choices.

At work

On any given day, over 140 million Americans are at work, so at least 140 million meals are eaten in the company cafeteria, at the desk, or at the construction site.

What you can do:

✓ Avoid fast-food breakfasts. They're not very healthy options, and fast food corporations rely on monoculture, long-distance transport, and over-packaging.

✓ Brown bag your meals and snacks more often. Bring leftovers from home in reusable containers, or reuse a paper bag.

✓ If you have a microwave oven in your workplace, reheat some leftovers brought from home.

✓ Recycle. This may mean carrying a bag or can until you find a proper bin.

✓ Encourage the company cafeteria to serve green and vegetarian options, and then select them.

✓ Order healthy foods for long meetings and stock the office fridge with fruit and other fresh snacks.

At play

Not at work or at home? Maybe you're enjoying yourself somewhere else. Theme parks log over 300 million visits a year, where people spend $9.1 billion, much of it on food. At professional sport events, people buy meals, drinks, and snacks. The 221 accredited zoos and aquariums in this country log over 175 million visits a year.

What you can do:

✓ When buying a small item (such as one muffin), tell the clerk you don't need a bag.

✓ At theme parks, ballparks, or zoo cafes, choose vegetarian options.

✓ Don't buy more than you'll eat. If you have some left over, share it or take it with you.

✓ At parties where disposable cups are used, write people's names on them so each guest needs only one cup throughout the event.

✓ At picnics, use reusable containers and dispose of trash properly.

Take me out to the food fair

One recent June, the equivalent of a sustainable county fair was held at McCovey Cove, near San Francisco's baseball park. The Giants teamed up with the Center for Urban Education about Sustainable Agriculture (CUESA) to host the event, which featured demonstrations on container gardening, beekeeping, composting, mushroom growing, healthful cooking, and more. Dave Stockdale, CUESA's director, told me that the event was "an homage to an old-fashioned county fair with contests, exhibits, demonstrations, animals, set against the backdrop of the carnival that the San Francisco Giants were operating." Naturally there had to be a competitive element in an event co-sponsored by an athletic team, so at noon there was a cherry-pit-spitting contest.

On the road

We travel for leisure, for education, and for work. Conferences, for example, are a multi-billion-dollar-a-year industry, whether for Star Trek fans or professional associations. What an opportunity for greening our food! Here's one example: Bioneers is an organization that supports inventive ways of living lightly on the Earth. Every

October it holds a major conference attended by thousands of people. At a televised satellite broadcast in Massachusetts, Bioneers organizers bought most conference food locally, composted the leftovers, and recycled. China dinnerware was used, rather than paper or plastic. Used cooking oil was sent to a nearby technical college for its biodiesel program.

What you can do:
✓ Bring your own snacks. Reuse glass jars to pack your drinks.
✓ Use only the amount of wrapping that your meal really needs.
✓ Avoid bottled water. Find a drinking fountain or bring a water container from home.
✓ Encourage your professional association to think of the Earth when planning its conferences.

Coffee, Wine, and Other Beverages

One day, wine lover Tyler Colman began to wonder about the impact of wine on the environment. He was pleasantly surprised to find that the main problems were not the fertilizers used to grow the grapes or the fermentation process, which produces the greenhouse gas carbon dioxide. The big problem? Transportation. In the U.S., 95% of domestic wine is grown on the west coast, but over two thirds of the population lives east of the Mississippi. Trucking wines across country in heavy glass bottles creates the heavy carbon footprint.

Other beverages have environmental impacts, too. Carbonated water may come from a natural source, but it involves packaging and trucking. Fruit juice may come from fruit grown with chemicals and transported long distances. Regional franchises bottle the national brands of sodas, so there is less of a transportation problem, but aluminum cans are made of ore extracted at great cost, and we don't recycle all the cans we use. (The U.S. still gets about 60% of its aluminum from virgin ore, at 20 times the energy needed to recycle aluminum). Sodas have no nutritional value and many of them have artificial dyes and sweeteners.

Coffee is grown far away, processed chemically, and full of caffeine, which can be addictive to some people. The average U.S. coffee drinker consumes three cups a day, which over a year adds up to 50 gallons made from 27 pounds of beans, representing the production of 20 to 30 coffee plants. Growers apply 11 pounds of fertilizer and a few ounces of pesticide to the plants for this one person. After harvest and processing, 43 pounds of coffee pulp go into local rivers, where it decomposes, taking up oxygen that fish need. Diesel-powered bean crushers are used to process the beans, and freighters using petroleum fuel bring them to the United States, where the roasting process burns natural gas. The final product is packaged in four-layer bags made of polyethylene, nylon, aluminum, and polyester.

On coffee plantations, trees are cut down to make room for coffee plants. Biologists in Mexico found that traditional shade coffee plantations supported 180 species of birds, but fewer than 20 bird species in sun fields. Without birds, insects multiply, so more pesticides are used, as well as fertilizers. Sun coffee fields thus contribute to species loss, land erosion, water pollution, and health risks to workers. Fortunately, shade-grown coffee is a growing niche. One third of America's coffee market consists of specialty coffees sold at higher prices if they taste better or are grown with the Earth and workers in mind.

What you can do:
✓ Buy organic, fair trade, and shade-grown coffee.
✓ Use unbleached coffee filters.
✓ Try herbal tea.
✓ Buy in bulk.
✓ Reuse and then recycle the container.
✓ Try soy, almond, and grain beverages.
✓ Try diverse fruit juices—organic, of course.
✓ Encourage small regional juice makers, not just national brands.
✓ Make a quart of your favorite tea and keep it chilled in your fridge.
✓ Avoid bottled water.

PART III
The Green Foodprint at Home

Cooking, serving, and cleaning up in your own kitchen can be made Earth-friendly. In this section, I've collected ways to save water and energy, and show you how to make the most of your food.

> The kitchen is the center of our homes–like the center of a wheel around which all revolves. The kitchen is also the center of a greater community, the hub from which many connections radiate to the world at large.
>
> —Annie Berthold Bond, author of
> *The Green Kitchen Handbook*

Use Energy Skillfully

The refrigerator is the biggest single user of household energy and generating the electricity to power the fridge emits carbon dioxide. Hydrofluorocarbons (HFCs), the chemicals that cool refrigerators, are greenhouse gases, contributing to global warming. So buying an energy-efficient fridge is one of the smartest moves you can make. Look for the Energy Star label (from the EPA and the Department of Energy), which indicates energy-efficient appliances, office equipment, computers, lighting, and more. In 2006 alone, Energy Star helped us reduce greenhouse gas emissions equivalent to 25 million vehicles, while saving $14 billion on energy bills.

The modern kitchen is also filled with coffee makers, grinders, blenders, and microwave ovens. Sometimes we use them wastefully, heating a large oven to heat a single muffin or using a special gadget to warm sandwiches on both sides. Energy-efficient appliances and microwave ovens can reduce waste. A microwave oven uses less power than a full-sized oven, cooking faster and letting you cook and serve in the same dish. This means using less hot water and soap for cleanup.

Refrigerator: What you can do:
- ✓ Don't buy a bigger refrigerator than you need. Buy an energy-efficient one, preferably from a manufacturer that will take back your fridge when you are done with it in order to recover the coolant and other materials.
- ✓ Fill the fridge less than three quarters full to allow cool air to circulate. Check the door seals for leaks. Replace the gasket (the rubber seal around the door) if necessary.
- ✓ Brush or vacuum the refrigerator coils once a year, so the refrigerator cools more efficiently.
- ✓ Set the temperature at 38 to 42 degrees F, and the freezer at 0 to 5 degrees F.
- ✓ Cover foods and liquids. This keeps food from drying

out and saves the fridge from having to work to remove moisture.

✓ Most hot foods can be safely cooled on the counter before being put in the fridge or freezer.

Oven: What you can do:

✓ Consider buying a convection oven, whose fan distributes the heat evenly and speeds the cooking process.

✓ Don't preheat the oven, unless the food requires a high temperature and a short (or precisely measured) cooking time.

✓ Use the smallest oven you have (or a toaster oven) for each task.

✓ After you turn off the oven, use the leftover heat to warm up rolls or dessert, to dry dishes, or (in winter) to heat the kitchen.

✓ Try a solar oven.

Solar ovens

Solar ovens are small, lightweight metal boxes that focus the sun's rays to bake bread, potatoes, rice, and more. A solar oven makes a good part of your emergency kit, too, in case of power outages or natural disaster. Solar ovens are being sent to developing countries, so that people there won't have to chop down trees to make cooking fires.

Stovetop: What you can do:

✓ Cover pots while cooking. This reduces energy use by two thirds.

✓ Electric burners can be turned off a few minutes before the end of the scheduled cooking time. The unit is still hot and continues cooking the food.

✓ Clean the reflector pans under the stovetop heating elements so heat reflects back to the pan.

✓ Use a pan the same size or a little bigger than the heating unit. If the pan is too large or too small, heat is wasted.

✓ Electric kettles and microwaves are efficient for heating small amounts of water.

✓ Enjoy more raw fresh foods (fruit, nuts, salads) that require no cooking at all.

Raw main courses?

Salads and fruits are just the beginning. Ingenious folks have invented ways to prepare raw appetizers, main courses, drinks, sauces, and desserts. Some dishes require electricity to run a blender, dehydrator, or juicer, but no gas or electricity is used to bake, boil, sauté, or steam them. I've tried raw mock salmon pate, date nut torte, vegetables sushi, and angel hair "pasta" with marinara sauce. They were delicious.

Dishwasher: What you can do:

✓ Run the dishwasher only when it is full. Use shorter cycles.

✓ Turn off the dishwasher after the final rinse and open the door slightly to air dry the dishes. This saves up to half the electricity used in a complete cycle.

✓ Wash the largest items by hand, leaving room in the dishwasher for many small items.

Other energy savers: What you can do:

✓ Use an instant hot water appliance installed at your sink. It's as efficient as boiling water on the stove.

✓ Don't wrap baked potatoes in aluminum foil. Cut them in half and microwave them face down on a plate, or simply bake them unwrapped.

✓ Steam corn on the cob instead of boiling it. This uses less water and heating fuel. It's faster and best of all, the corn tastes better.

✓ If you eat meat, cook it in small pieces rather than whole roasts or birds. This uses less fuel.

Use Water Wisely

Water is more precious than gold. We can't live without it, yet we are rapidly exhausting our supplies, due to overpopulation, over-consumption, pollution, waste, and agriculture. Our water footprint is dangerously large. Agriculture uses two thirds of the water being drawn from rivers, lakes, and aquifers—twice as much water as all buildings, industry, and mining combined. Huge amounts of water are needed to grow crops for animals and to water the animals themselves.

- Manure and runoff of pesticides, hormones, and antibiotics contaminate our waters, wasting almost as much water as that we actually use.
- The American Water Works Association estimates that nearly 14% of household water is wasted by leaks.
- We are dipping into underground water, some of which was deposited eons ago as "fossil water." The Ogallala aquifer, a huge reservoir under eight states which provides water for 20% of America's irrigated land, is being depleted so much that in places the groundwater level has dropped 150 feet.

What you can do:

- ✓ Keep a bottle of drinking water in the fridge so you won't run the tap to get cool water.
- ✓ Fix leaky faucets. Hot water leaks are doubly costly, since you're also paying for heating. To find out how much water a leak is wasting, use the calculator at awwa.org/awwa/waterwiser/dripcalc.cfm.
- ✓ Don't turn on the tap and then wander around the kitchen peeking in the fridge or looking for dishes to wash. Soap up your hands before turning on the tap for hand-washing.
- ✓ Use less water to boil pasta. Tradition says 6 quarts; 2 is plenty.

✓ Eat less meat, or none. It takes 5 to 10 times as much water to produce a pound of meat as it does a pound of wheat.
✓ Steam or microwave vegetables instead of boiling them. This uses less water, preserves vitamins, and makes food taste better.

Is washing dishes by hand more environmentally friendly than using a dishwasher? It depends. When you're washing by hand, do you let the hot water run incessantly? Do you use so much soap that you have to use a lot of water to rinse it off? Do you let dishes sit for days before washing them, so that the food has crusted and requires repeated washing? All these mean you're not washing efficiently. Meanwhile, a dishwasher filled completely and run on an energy-conserving cycle can actually be efficient. The U.S. Department of Energy calculated that doing the dishes by hand with the water running uses almost 6,000 gallons of water a year. An efficient dishwasher, on the other hand, would use less than 900 gallons.

What you can do:
✓ Don't pre-wash your dishes; just scrape them before putting them in the dishwasher. Soak heavily soiled ones first, if necessary.
✓ Don't let the faucet run at high volume while rinsing dishes one at a time.
✓ Compost food scraps instead of spending water and electricity to put them down the disposal.
✓ Run the dishwasher only when it's full.

Meanwhile, south of the border
A Goldman Environmental Prize, the annual equivalent of the Nobel, was awarded in 2008 to Jesus Leon, who has run a nonprofit for 25 years in his native Mexico. Leon's group in the Mixtec Highlands builds rainwater storage structures and organic composting systems and planted a million new trees to reforest 2,471 acres of land. They also revive contour ditches that were built over 500 years ago to catch rainfall.

Use Only Good Gadgets

Some kitchen tools are indispensable, some are useful, and some are toys. Gadgets save labor by using electricity to chop, puree, or cook things slowly or quickly or in a specialized way. Some gadgets seem designed to save muscle power, on the assumption that manual labor is somehow demeaning. But then we go to the gym to use other fancy machines to build up our muscles. When you chop vegetables and open cans with a hand can opener, you are using less electricity and moving your body.

Every manufactured object also contains energy from materials embedded in the object itself: wood, metal, plastic, glass, paint, and petroleum. Manufacturing also requires energy to dig the ore and to heat, mix, and shape the materials. Finally, natural resources are used to package and transport products through distribution channels to your home.

Embedded energy exists in all products, from cars to can openers, so choose your gadgets wisely. Pressure cookers (with tight-fitting lids that allow water to be superheated above 212 degrees) do save energy. But manufacturing a new one involves embedded energy, so be sure you'll actually use it before investing in one. Or get a used one at a garage sale or thrift shop.

Some kitchen gadgets are really toys for grownups: microwaveable ice cream scoops, for instance. If your ice cream is so hard that you can't scoop it, your freezer is too cold. Electric pepper mills, cherry pitting devices, microwave s'more makers—I've even seen advertisements for a home cotton candy making machine, a weirdly shaped pan that bakes brownies with more edges, and a gadget whose sole function is to cut up a hot dog to look like an octopus.

Do you really need such things? Are they really welcome as gifts? Electric can openers are a bit more sensible, and valuable for those with physical impairments. But how often do you use an avocado knife, a pineapple slicer, or that heavy pile of metal called a waffle iron? Think how many gadgets gather dust in the backs of cabinets, waiting till the day they are set out for the garage sale.

What you can do:

✓ Use the smallest practical appliance without compromising safety.

✓ Single-task appliances, such as waffle irons, should be purchased only if you are sure you will use them regularly.

✓ Use a water filter (a pitcher or a device that attaches to your tap). After you recoup the initial embedded energy, the filter will save the resources that would be used to produce, package, and transport bottled water.

✓ Check the Energy Star ratings for the energy efficiency of appliances.

✓ Buy some gadgets second-hand.

✓ Take care of your appliances so they last longer.

Enjoy Leftovers

Food that reaches your table represents planting, watering, outwitting the competition (bugs also want that berry or grain of wheat), harvesting, saving seeds for next year, packing, shipping, and marketing. If you've grown food yourself, you know the time and attention that went into it.

Leftover performance art can help the Earth. That untouched potato, half a cup of pasta sauce, and last half of a zucchini could be part of a wonderful soup. The French call it "pot au feu"—the pot on the fire where leftovers go for their next incarnation. It's fun. You end up with dishes that are never exactly the same and you get to exercise your creativity.

The way you store leftovers can also help the Earth. Aluminum foil and cling wrap do save food, but the raw materials are extracted, manufactured, packaged, transported, and discarded. So look at foil and wrap as the valuable commodities they are, not trash to be used once and thrown away.

What you can do:
✓ Learn some new recipes.
✓ Consider the European custom—buy smaller amounts of fresh produce, and do so more often. Walk to the store. Less produce is wasted and you get exercise and social contact.
✓ Put leftovers in a bowl and invert a saucer on top, using no foil or wrap.
✓ If you use aluminum foil, use it repeatedly before recycling it.
✓ Store several items together—rice and vegetables, potatoes and beans—to minimize the use of foil and plastic.
✓ Use empty jars to store leftovers.

Reduce Waste

The amount of food we waste annually is staggering—over 90 *billion* pounds of food a year. During World War II, it was considered patriotic to use everything thriftily, from food to gasoline to clothing. More than 20,000 committees and 400,000 volunteers organized to recycle metal, rubber, and other materials.

We realized then that natural resources were precious. They still are. That includes the last few slices of bread in a loaf, the other half of the onion, the last cup of soup. The clever cook works these into the next meal. Marvelous dishes have been born of necessity.

And don't forget the invisible ingredient in every food. "Virtual water" consists of all the water that is in a product or went into producing it. One cup of coffee thrown away took 37 gallons of water to grow, package, and transport. One egg took 53 gallons. Reducing food waste saves water. Even the end of the food journey—what's left after every bit of usable food has been eaten—can help restore the Earth. Put peels and plate scraps into the compost pile. Put water from cooking vegetables onto the houseplants. Your kitchen becomes a way-station in the great cycle of life.

What you can do:

✓ Don't be afraid of small imperfections. Most blemishes on fresh produce do not affect its taste or nutritional value. A tiny dot of mold on bread can be cut away.

✓ If you buy produce on sale, it's probably at the peak of ripeness and about to go bad soon. Eat it right away.

✓ Check your fridge's crisper drawer so you remember what's there. Use fresh produce promptly.

✓ Give yourself smaller servings. Tune in to your stomach: how hungry are you, really?

Share the Bounty

So you've saved leftovers for creative reuse and sent scraps and peels to the compost. Is there anything more you can do? You could help hungry people in your community.

- There are a billion hungry people, one out of every six people on Earth. Many are children.
- Millions of Americans have to choose between paying for food and paying for utilities, rent, or medical care.

Much of this hunger is preventable. Huge amounts of food get lost in the cracks of distribution. In the back of your cupboard, cans of food are probably nearing their expiration date. A food bank could use them.

There are millions of fruit trees in this country, and many of them are not being fully harvested. Remember the ancient concept of gleaning? At harvest time, farmers left some of the crop in the field so hungry people could gather it. Nowadays, local organizations (such as Second Harvest) will come to your house and collect the apples and pears that might otherwise go to waste.

What you can do:
- ✓ Donate canned goods and unopened baked goods to local food banks or to holiday food drives.
- ✓ Contact Second Harvest or other gleaning organization to gather the crops from your fruit trees that might otherwise be wasted.
- ✓ Harvest your own trees and donate any excess you won't use.
- ✓ Patronize restaurants that donate to food banks.

Clean Up Harmlessly

Cleaning up after meals can be hard on the Earth if you use a lot of paper towels and harsh cleansers. Paper towels can be handy, but I've seen people tear off a sheet, use it to wipe up a few drops of spilled tea, and throw it away. The same for napkins. If a family of four used cloth napkins instead of paper at every meal for a year, they would save 4,380 paper napkins from the landfill. There is some laundering involved, but cloth napkins reduce your family's trash and help the Earth.

Paper towels with recycled content are available. If every household in America replaced one roll of 180-sheet two-ply virgin fiber paper towels with a 100% recycled one, we would save 864,000 trees, 3.4 million cubic feet of landfill (3,900 full garbage trucks), and 354 million gallons of water (a year's supply for 10,100 families of four).

Common harsh cleansers are full of phosphorus, chemicals, perfumes, dyes, and abrasive powders. Alternatives are available. Seventh Generation, which makes Earth-friendly household goods, was voted #1 Best Company on the Planet because of its excellent performance in environment, human rights, community involvement, animal protection, and other issues.

Or you could devise your own cleansers. Baking soda, vinegar, and ammonia can be used to clean many things. Home hygiene expert Annie Berthold Bond maintains that five basic materials will clean everything: baking soda, washing soda, distilled white vinegar, vegetable-based liquid soap, and tea tree oil. Don't leave foods or food scraps lying around—they can attract critters. If you need to get rid of some unwanted critters, don't use poison. The rodents who eat the poisons may die outside, and then wild animals such as hawks are poisoned by eating them.

What you can do:
- ✓ Buy Earth-friendly cleaning materials.
- ✓ Or make your own. Combine half a cup of white vinegar with enough water to make a gallon. This can be used to clean dishes, coffeepots, etc. Baking soda is a good abrasive for appliances, cutting boards, and sinks, and it deodorizes at the same time.
- ✓ If a pan has burned-on food, soak it before scrubbing. For badly charred stainless steel pots, pour in full-strength vinegar and let it stand for several days.
- ✓ Place a scrubber in the pan and use the end of a wooden spoon handle to press the scrubber against the burned-on food. This concentrates the scrubbing force of your arm and makes cleaning up fast and easy.
- ✓ Instead of using harsh oven cleaner chemicals and a huge jolt of electricity, clean oven spills with baking soda and steel wool before they harden.
- ✓ Avoid soaps that have antibiotics.
- ✓ If a drain is clogged, use a plumber's snake or plunger instead of harsh chemicals to clear it.
- ✓ Prevent oven spills; clean them up promptly when they occur.
- ✓ Clean up countertop spills with a cloth, not paper towels.
- ✓ If you use paper towels and napkins, buy ones that have a high percentage of recycled material and minimal bleaching. Then you can put soiled ones in the compost.

Maximize Materials by Recycling

You're probably already recycling some of the paper, aluminum, steel, glass, and plastic that comes into your life. But we can do better. When we throw things away, we turn land into junkyards, quaintly called "landfills," to store our discards.

- In 2005, the U.S. produced 245 million tons of municipal solid waste. That's 4.5 pounds per person per day.
- As of 2006, airports and airlines in the U.S. discard enough aluminum cans each year that 58 Boeing 747s could be built with them.

Recycling, a $238 billion business that employs over a million people, reduces this burden.

- Recycling and composting diverted 82 million tons of material from landfills in 2006.
- Some appliances are being recycled, taken back by their manufacturers and disassembled so the materials can be reused.

Recycling isn't perfect. Energy is used to move the material and process it. Supply and demand are not perfectly matched. But recycling is the most immediate and sensible way we can help lighten our load on the Earth.

Prevent hardening of the pipelines

San Francisco residents and restaurants were dumping 65,000 gallons of used cooking oil down their sinks, clogging the city's sewer system and costing $3.5 million a year to repair it. The city now collects used cooking oil and turns it into biofuel for fire trucks, buses, and ambulances. What a great way to keep the city's metal arteries clean!

What you can do:

- ✓ Recycle glass, aluminum, paper, newspaper, and plastic. This includes when you are at home, at work, outside, and at play.
- ✓ Carry bottles and cans home from office or ballpark if recycling bins are not in place there. Encourage management to get bins.
- ✓ Buy goods made from recycled materials—paper, fleece vests and parkas, shoes, garden tools, carpets and carpet pads, and more. This encourages manufacturers to buy the recycled material and turn it into new products.
- ✓ Eat less fast food, which creates paper waste. Bring lunch from home instead.
- ✓ If you do go to a fast food establishment, tell the manager you're concerned about recycling.
- ✓ Know your community's recycling services and make use of them.

Build Topsoil by Composting

The last stop on your food's march through your kitchen is the compost bin. America's topsoil, the layer of Earth in which we grow our crops, is being lost at an alarming rate. Topsoil is the stuff of life, the very source of plants on which humans and animals ultimately depend. Tons of precious earth are floating down the Mississippi River and our other rivers and streams or blowing away in the wind.

You can easily create topsoil. Once you start composting, you'll be amazed that you ever thought of food scraps as garbage. You could simply make a pile in the yard, but this might be hard to protect from your pets or other animals. Better, purchase a bin from the local hardware store or home supply warehouse. Some cities subsidize compost bins, making them available to residents at a discount. There are bin designs for every budget and level of interest. There's even a small one you can keep in the house.

Confessions of a wormophile

"I keep worms. I keep them in the backyard in a hinged box that people call a worm bin ... It is a chest of garden treasure, a microbial engine room, a guilt extinguisher and a bank for small deposits of virtue. The worms, you see, eat my garbage ... You bed them down in shredded newspaper, then add peels, pits, moldy things, coffee grounds ... The worms obliterate evidence of neglect, the things that provoke annoying pinpricks of kitchen guilt, and give you compost in return." Lawrence Downes in the *New York Times*

Your grass clippings and other yard waste can also go in the compost bin, and so can vacuum cleaner lint, wool and cotton rags, sawdust, wilted flowers, biodegradable plates and utensils, and fireplace ashes. Properly tended, a compost heap can turn this material into new soil in a few weeks. To speed the process, you can add some nitrogen-rich manure purchased from the hardware store, stir the heap occasionally, and put in some worms. These trusty creatures gobble up the leftovers and turn them into dirt. Compost aficionados describe the fine points of layering, nitrogen concentration, moisture levels, and turning frequency. You can do all that, but it isn't required. Time alone will eventually turn your scraps into black gold.

> Do the rot thing.
>
> —The Alameda County (California)
> Waste Management Authority

Composting is an easy, inexpensive way to renew the Earth. Your trash bill might go down if a smaller garbage can will now fit your needs. With your home-made dirt, you can improve the soil on your property or give it away to friends. And you'll have the satisfaction of knowing you are returning to the age-old cycle of soil to food to soil.

What you can do:
- ✓ See if your community offers subsidized compost bins for sale to its residents.
- ✓ Save potato peels, apple cores, banana peels, and soggy lettuce leaves—all those things that never make it to your table. You can buy a crock, or use an empty milk carton.
- ✓ Add the scrapings from your plates after meals.
- ✓ If you have your own bin, drop the scraps into your compost bin and cover it. If your community collects food waste, put your scraps in the collection bin.

**PART
IV**

PART IV
Join the Movement

All kinds of people are shifting to Earth-friendly living: students, architects, activists, homemakers, legislators, doctors, surfers, internet designers, artists, photographers, chefs, schoolchildren, and more. Some love nature, some are devoted to social justice, some care about animals, some are concerned about the world they are leaving to their children and grandchildren. Spiritual values motivate many of us, whether we call it Earth stewardship, religious environmentalism, or green spirituality. Others find creative and economic opportunity as new inventions and services are needed.

> Suddenly everywhere I look, I see people eagerly
> reclaiming control of their food systems.
>
> —Novelist Barbara Kingsolver, author of
> *Animal, Vegetable, Miracle*

Sustainable and More Humane Agriculture

Michigan grower Jim Koan saw his organic apples threatened by a beetle that eats apples that fall too early to the ground. Koan brought in four pigs to scarf up the infested apples. The pigs successfully interrupted the beetles' life cycle. They also eat pulp left over from the farm's cider operation. This solution was efficient and Earth-friendly.

> Unlike industrial agriculture, which looks at the farm as an outdoor factory with inputs entering at one end and outputs exiting the other, sustainable agriculture views a farm as an integrated system made up of elements like soil, plants, insects, and animals.
> —Michael Brower and Warren Leon,
> Union of Concerned Scientists

Sustainable agriculture uses ancient and modern techniques to make farming safer.

No-till technology. Instead of plowing fields with huge machines that compact the soil or disperse it to be blown away by the wind, sustainable farmers plant narrower rows, causing 90% less erosion, better water filtration, and more soil diversity. No-till methods raise yields, improve soil quality, and help keep carbon in the ground instead of in the air.

Integrated pest management (IPM). Instead of blanketing the land with huge sprays of chemicals, sustainable farmers use natural solutions, with synthetic chemicals only as a last resort. Sustainable farmers rotate crops, plant native grasses under trees, let natural predators handle pests, and tolerate a few harmless weeds.

Rotating crops with animals. Animals are brought in to churn up the soil, deposit fertilizer, and eliminate pests. Sustainable farmers may bring in goats to eat weeds, and geese to eat insects.

Companion planting. Fields are planted in beneficial pairings: spinach with strawberries, or carrots with onions. One plant may provide nutrients the other needs, or protect it from pests. In agroforestry, trees are planted with other crops growing below. The crop produces a regular income for the landowner while the trees are growing large enough to sell.

Pastured animals. Chickens and cattle live outside, eating their natural diets, and are not crowded and vulnerable to epidemics. Pastured (grass-fed) cattle are not fed the corn diet that uses up the corn harvest and that gives the cows digestive disorders (for which CAFO operators give them antibiotics). Pastured chickens get real access to outdoors, in outdoor pens that are towed around the fields to bring them to new areas.

Knowing the fine points. Computers help calculate how much water a plant needs and is getting, precisely aiming sprinklers, and other methods. Earth-damaging practices are made obsolete by making small changes in timing or placing seeds, and by companion planting.

Three other philosophies of farming are catching on. *Biodynamic* farming is a set of simple, natural techniques being used to produce crops, dairy, and even wine. Fetzer's Ceago Vinegarden in Clear Lake, California, uses biodynamic methods. Pests are eaten by chickens, who give the vineyard a sideline in certified humanely raised eggs. *Permaculture* involves intimate knowledge of one's land, and directing water and airflow to cultivate diversity and resilience. *Biointensive* farming is a system for getting the most food value from the smallest amount of land by building up healthy soil, deeply dug plots, companion planting, and other hands-on skills.

There's another benefit of sustainable agriculture. When food is grown without tons of chemicals, which can drift on the wind or leach into creeks and groundwater, people can live nearby. This allows farmers to coexist with suburbanites, rather than being driven off the land as the population spreads. One farm of 5-10 acres could feed 200 to 300 families.

To sum up, sustainable agriculture is an exciting blend of new technology and revived traditions that work hand in hand to produce food in a more Earth-friendly way.

What you can do:
- ✓ Buy organic food as often as you can.
- ✓ Investigate Community Supported Agriculture.
- ✓ Pay attention to labels.

More humane treatment of animals

In CAFOs (confined animal feeding operations), thousands of cows and chickens spend their lives overcrowded in miserable conditions, destined for cruel slaughterhouses. I'm glad to report that this, too, is changing, thanks to the efforts of dedicated activists and organizations—though not changing quickly enough to save billions of animals from suffering. You can help by seeking more humanely produced meat, dairy, and eggs (if you eat these foods), labelled "pastured" or "certified humane" or "100% grass fed."

But beware. I'll say it again: words like "natural" and "free range" have been watered down. Agribusiness's cynical use of loopholes and hair-splitting means that a so-called "free-range" operation may be really a barn with ten thousand chickens, where one small door leading to a small plot outside is open one hour a day or leads to a barren lot that no self-respecting chicken would visit.

What you can do:

✓ If you eat beef, choose beef from "100% grass-fed" cows.

✓ Buy organic eggs, which by definition come from hens that are raised more humanely.

✓ Patronize restaurants that use more humanely raised meat.

✓ Eat less meat, dairy, and eggs—or none.

✓ If you do eat meat, visit these sites to find humanely raised meat, dairy, and eggs.

- eatwellguide.org
- localharvest.org
- animalwelfareapproved.org

Food Professionals

Maybe you are—or hope to be—a food professional: someone who cooks, runs a restaurant, writes a food column, or teaches cooking classes. You may have wondered if there's more you can do to encourage the food revolution. Yes, there is.

Chefs

Chefs Collaborative is a non-profit with over 1,000 members—chefs, culinary school instructors, managers of large food service operations, distributors, owners of specialty stores, farmers, fishers, and ranchers. By changing their food choices and educating diners nationwide, this group works to make sustainability second nature for food professionals.

Wolfgang Puck leads a multi-million-dollar empire of restaurants and frozen foods. A few years ago Puck said, "I have had a change of heart. I want to be more outspoken about the treatment of animals ... In all my restaurants, catering businesses, licensed foods and takeout establishments, I'm committed to using organic ingredients and humanely raised meats and fish." Think of the enormous impact this one man's decision has made!

Restaurateurs

Restaurant owners have power, too. Alice Waters, the famed restaurateur of Chez Panisse in Berkeley, California, created the Edible Schoolyard, where kids can learn about caring for the land and feeding their families and communities. On a vacant lot, kids began growing food and soon a garden classroom and a kitchen classroom were added. Waters says, "The table is where people communicate, where culture is passed on from generation to generation ... They are learning to take care of the land, they are learning to feed themselves, they are learning how to communicate at the table." Some ingenious and hard-working folks have reversed the trend toward specialization and formed all-in-one ventures—growing fine organic produce, cooking it, and serving it in their own restaurants–"vertical integration" in the food world.

Urban agriculture

Urban agriculture is an informal nationwide movement of people finding ways to use back yards and unused land to grow food. You could start a back yard farm or become a gardening coach to show others how to turn their weedy land into well-tended gardens. Or you could be a traveling farmer, doing all the work in customers' back yards, charging fees to plant and maintain the garden, and giving (or sharing with) the landowners the fresh produce. Vacant city lots have been converted to gardens. Other city dwellers rent land at a small price from their cities. They can make real money:

- Added Value Farm in Brooklyn started out as a 3-acre asphalt ball field. In its fourth year of operation, the youth group sold over $25,000 worth of food.
- Growing Power, a nonprofit in Milwaukee, operates one acre and grossed over $220,000 in 2007.

Kids plant their own pumpkin patch

In Lafayette, California, a dozen children, their parents, and a resident cat took part in the creation of their very own pumpkin patch. At a home that is part of the Urban Farmers project, the back yard was cleared, hoed, and prepared with drip irrigation. Then the party began. Siamack Sioshansi, co-creator of the project, explained to the children how seeds grow into seedlings and then into plants and finally into pumpkins. After a lively question-and-answer period, kids planted their seeds and feasted on watermelons and cookies. A few weeks later, a scarecrow-making party was held, showing kids how to protect their crops–in a charming low-tech way.

Master gardeners

A master gardener has taken courses and earned a certificate in gardening. This can be a rewarding career—and a way to give back. In 2003, master gardeners in Colorado donated 53,000 hours of volunteer time to extension and horticultural programs in 21 counties. That year master gardeners in Illinois and Missouri donated 140,000 pounds of food to community hunger projects, participating in the Plant a Row for the Hungry Program. Wisconsin has over 1,000 master gardeners, who volunteered 74,000 hours to projects such as building community gardens and training for immigrant families.

Authors and journalists

Writers propel the food revolution, which was named by John Robbins in his book *The Food Revolution*. John's earlier book, *Diet for a New America*, sparked the movement for conscious food choices. Pioneer Frances Moore Lappé (*Diet for a Small Planet*) changed the way millions of Americans think about food, environment, justice, and compassion. Michael Pollan has published best-selling books on food: *The Botany of Desire, The Omnivore's Dilemma*, and *In Defense of Food*. Marion Nestle, nutritionist and expert on government policy, published *Food Politics: How the Food Industry Influences Nutrition and Health, Safe Food,* and *What to Eat*. Eric Schlosser's investigative book *Fast Food Nation* awoke us to the damage the fast food industry wreaks on people, animals, and the Earth. For a sobering yet hilarious account of the real world of ranching written by a former cattle rancher, check out Howard Lyman's book *Mad Cowboy: Plain Truth from the Cattle Rancher Who Won't Eat Meat*. These writers helped inspire the popular documentary *Food Inc.* Regional magazines and newspapers also have food columns and, increasingly, environmental columns.

Teachers

Whether you teach cooking or nutrition at a school, college, or community center, you are influencing the minds of eaters. You can show them the value of organic, the ways to use diverse fruits and vegetables, and the value of locally grown food. Science teachers can make food a focus for lessons in botany, biology, chemistry, and more. Humane educators teach children and adults how to live with compassion and wisdom, respecting humans, animals, and diverse cultures. Elementary school teachers can incorporate lessons about plants, animals, sunshine, farms, and food into their classes.

Good food–pass it on.

Every good movement reaches out to young people, including the food revolution now under way. To find classes, websites, interactive games, teacher resource guides, fact sheets, activity ideas, and more, visit the California Foundation for Agriculture In the Classroom, cfaitc.org. A charming calendar on the website tells you about things like ... get ready for it ... National Mustard Day. If Mustard Day is not for you, there are other food holidays all year 'round, including "Sneak Some Zucchini onto Your Neighbor's Porch Day." (This book is not responsible for minor acts of reverse vegetable vandalism).

Beekeepers

Bees, like birds and bats, pollinate our crops. The collapse of millions of beehives in recent years has alarmed experts and raised the profile—and importance—of beekeepers. Surprisingly, urban areas are well suited to the beekeeping profession. There is probably a beekeepers' organization near you.

Did you know that Sir Edmund Hillary was a professional beekeeper? He and sherpa Tenzing Norgay were the first mountain climbers to reach the top of Mt. Everest.

Vintners

Sixty-eight U.S. vineyards are certified biodynamic or transitioning to biodynamic. Other labels certify that a wine is organic or fair trade. Wine bottles are being made lighter, using less glass and gasoline to transport. At one of the greenest vineyards I know, Medlock Ames, a solar array provides the electricity. The owners encourage barn owls, hawks, and bats to handle rodents and other unwanted creatures. Sheep eat the weeds and turn them into natural fertilizer, while geese munch pond algae. Instead of installing high fences to keep out wildlife (deer, wild pigs, and bobcats), the owners have created migration corridors so animals can move through their land without harming the vines. So there's plenty of room for sustainable activity in the wine business.

Nutritionists and doctors

Nutritionists do a lot of educating and also have clinical duties: designing the menus for schools, hospitals, and nursing homes; counseling people with eating disorders; and helping people with diet-related medical problems such as diabetes and heart conditions. Doctors Neal Barnard (head of Physicians Committee for Responsible Medicine) and Dean Ornish, among others, have campaigned tirelessly to alert us to the health benefits of fresh, organic, plant-based diets.

Farmers

Let's not forget the most important people of all—the ones who grow our food. Thousands who raised food for us are now reaching retirement age. In the U.S., the average age of farmers is 57, and fewer young people are joining the field, according to the USDA. So when these farmers retire, who's going to grow our food? And if urban sprawl takes over all the remaining farmland near cities, where will they do it? We need a new generation of people to grow food. Maybe you? Someone you love?

With community supported agriculture, urban agriculture, and the other trends you've read about in this book, there's a variety of farming methods in the new food world. Learning to grow living things has been particularly meaningful for some military veterans returning from war. Said one, "I think a lot of the depression in the military spawns from not having a purpose. In the military, if you get into an altercation, your life is defined by tragedy. [Now] my life is defined by growing and harvesting things." A Nebraska program called "Combat Boots to Cowboy Boots" helps returning veterans transition to farming and ranching.

An acre or two can be incredibly productive, especially if it is used to grow a variety of crops. Community Supported Agriculture can make these ventures a success. Small artisanal creameries are also building a following for their distinctive, flavorful batches of butter, yogurt, and cheese. In "agro-tourism," farmers take in paying guests— a dude ranch with vegetables!

The food pro smorgasbord

Off-beat food careers are now arising. San Francisco journalist Ilana deBare discovered a company that teaches cooking inside corporations as a form of team building; tour guides who lead tours of farmers' markets and artisan bakeries; and prep kitchens where you can go for recipes and all the ingredients for a meal you prepare and take home. Experts in biodynamic and permaculture farming can become consultants. Mark Smallwood is the "green mission specialist" at Whole Foods in the Washington, DC, area. One of his many tasks is to encourage people to grow their own food. What? A company that urges its own customers to become the competition? This must be the new food world.

The town that was saved by food

Hardwick, Vermont, was in trouble. The largest employers had left and the town was in decline. Rather than give up, residents got creative, starting or expanding food and farming businesses. One small company went from 5 to 350 customers for its tofu made from locally grown soybeans. The farmers' market and community gardens are expanding. The University of Vermont helps with marketing, research, and transportation. Two brothers who had been making award-winning cheese began to do the aging process for other cheesemakers and recently opened new aging caves with space for 2 million pounds of cheese. A man with a seed-collecting hobby now has a million-dollar business selling seeds nationwide. The local CSA has 200 participants, who pump their food dollars into local farms. The Vermont Food Venture Center (where growers can rent kitchens to add value to their produce) is moving to Hardwick from a nearby city. All told, about 100 jobs have been added to the local economy in the last few years. Not bad for a town of 3,000 people.

Growing Your Food

Jo Murphy, a student at Wellesley College, recruited her fellow students to grow food on college land. One year they planted tomatoes, spinach, lettuce, hot peppers, eggplants, and more—including some "volunteer" pumpkins that came from seeds in the compost. They share their harvest with the student co-op café, the Red Cross, and local hunger relief organizations. Growing food, as these students found, can be gratifying in many ways. Most of them help the Earth.

- You know that what you've grown is organic.
- In your small plot, you won't cause the problems of monoculture.
- You can avoid genetically modified foods.
- Except for seeds and soil amendment, you're not using packaging, refrigeration, or gasoline for transport.
- A vegetable garden is the perfect place to use the compost you've been faithfully making.
- You can promote biodiversity by planting heritage varieties.
- You experience the creativity of helping something to grow.

I visited one modestly sized kitchen garden in the university town of Palo Alto, California, and found that on their small lot the homeowners grew many kinds of grain, vegetables, fruits, and nuts–19 crops in all.

Kids outstanding in their field

Schoolchildren in Albuquerque, New Mexico, got so excited after they toured Los Poblanos Organics farm that they wanted to farm, too. So Los Poblanos offered to let the kids grow food there. At harvest time, the children sold their produce at the local farmers' market. These kids belong to Roots and Shoots, the children's arm of the Jane Goodall Institute, which works worldwide to save wildlife and educate people about nature. Another chapter of Roots and Shoots in Yucca Valley, California, grew food with donated seeds and compostables from a nearby coffee shop.

Why grow food?

Growing food supports self-sufficiency. In wartime, it was a patriotic duty: during World War I, over 5 million "victory gardens" were planted, and during World War II, over 15 million. This idea is being revived. At the 2008 Slow Food Nation festival, volunteers planted a demonstration garden, with beets, lettuce, kale, wide range of greens, peas, beans, tomatoes, and squash. Naturally, they called it the Victory Garden.

Rising food prices make growing food seem like a sensible investment. It does take time, but maybe less than you think. A 10-gallon pot with one tomato plant could yield 20 pounds of tomatoes and requires only a few minutes a week to tend and water. Three zucchini plants could yield 15 to 20 pounds of food. This is bounty in plain sight—and many people are already harvesting it. Over 70% of all U.S. households (an estimated 82 million households) participated in lawn and garden activities in 2007.

Finally, remember biodiversity. Could your backyard apple tree be a rare variety that should be saved? Could you swap seeds of heirloom fruits and vegetables, and help to keep them from going extinct?

Authors and acorns

Oak trees produce hundreds of acorns every year, and politely drop them at our feet. This is food in plain sight. Here's my recipe for turning them into flour: Wrap an acorn in a towel (to prevent shell pieces from flying all over the kitchen), put it on a cutting board, take a hammer, and smite the acorn to break the shell. Repeat until you have about a quart of shelled acorns. Boil them for two hours, changing the water every twenty minutes. Drain the acorns, crumble them, and spread them out on metal pan for a day until they're dry, then run them through the food processor. Recipes using boiled acorns or acorn flour can be found on the internet, or you could invent your own.

Where to grow

Food can be grown in all sorts of places. City-dwellers grow tomatoes in pots or plant a plot in their back yards, and make sure to tend and harvest their fruit trees. Schools in California have been welcoming food gardens for years. Some communities have allotments for gardening on public land. Rooftop gardens make "farming in the sky" possible. In Brooklyn, a 6,000-square-foot roof farm grows food for local shops and restaurants.

The perk that grows on you

A Minneapolis public relations firm that has sustainable companies on its client list sponsors a garden where employees build camaraderie and morale by growing vegetables. Beans, beets, and pumpkins are among their crops. Said Haberman & Associates employee Renee Kelly, "There's a sense of calm out here. You can get away from the desk and the computer and get to know each other on a deeper level." Other corporations are adding gardens to their activities–in part because there's evidence that doing so is good for employees' health (thus reducing medical costs). I knew there was a bottom line in here somewhere..... In fact, this is a triple-bottom line victory, for people, planet, and the businesses that help their employees grow.

Colleges are coming on board. At Messiah College in Grantham, Pennsylvania, students planted a quarter-acre vegetable garden on campus, growing tomatoes, lettuce, watermelons, and snow peas, after attending a sustainable agriculture conference and talking to farmers. Volunteers sell the produce to staff and the dining hall and have a waiting list for their harvest. Meanwhile, over 650 presidents of colleges and universities have signed the American College and University Presidents' Climate Commitment, pledging to make their campuses climate neutral; food service is an important part of this campaign. At Northland College in Wisconsin, the cafeteria serves vegetarian and vegan choices, cage-free eggs, sustainable seafood, and organic food. Food scraps from cafeterias and dorms are turned into compost, which is used in the student-run campus vegetable garden. The cafeteria saves water by eliminating trays; this encourages diners to take less food, reducing waste.

Food from the fringe

Urban edge agriculture takes advantage of open land on the outskirts of cities. On one 18-acre site outside San Francisco, organic food is grown by six separate groups, including inner-city youth and Laotian immigrants. The land, owned by the San Francisco Public Utilities Commission, sits atop the pipeline that carries water from the Sierra Mountains to the city, and would otherwise go idle. Two of the six organizations sell their food to inner-city residents, who often have limited access to fresh, healthy food. Others sell their goods to restaurants, grow rare varieties, and feed their own families. Look around. How many acres of unused land can you find in your area?

What to grow

- Herbs: These are the easiest "crops" to grow for personal use. A few small pots inside your kitchen or outside your back door can provide basil, rosemary, sage, thyme, and more.
- Vegetables: Tomatoes, zucchini, peas, garlic, and climbing green beans are easy to grow. Corn requires larger plots but is delicious when fresh. Kale, chard, yellow crookneck squash, and collard greens are prolific and easy to grow.
- Salads: Besides lettuce (easy varieties to grow are oakleaf, red curly leaf, and black-seeded Simpson's), you could grow spinach, nasturtiums, arugula, Italian dandelion, mountain cress, leeks, onions, and mustard.
- Mushrooms: These are easy to grow, contain protein, and come in many varieties.

- Fruit trees: These add beauty and value to property—and also help the planet. A mature tree absorbs carbon dioxide from the air and adds oxygen. It offers shade on hot days. The bountiful harvest of delicious fruit almost seems like an extra.

How to grow

Soil fertility depends on organic matter, nutrients, minerals, insects, microbes, worms and other factors. You can enrich your soil with natural amendments, compost, and worms. You can even buy mushroom-based fertilizer. Of course you'll avoid chemical pesticides and herbicides. You'll water your plants by hand or use drip irrigation or other water-conserving methods. But what about bugs, deer, and other critters that would just love to eat your crops? The Earth-friendly gardener uses the following methods of natural pest control:

What you can do:

✓ Pick off insects by hand. In a small plot, this short task isn't burdensome and spares your land the pesticides which endanger children, pets and wildlife.

✓ Recall that some insects (ladybugs, beetles, spiders) are beneficial—another reason not to douse your place with chemicals. To attract beneficial insects, plant parsley, dill, and sunflowers.

✓ Remember that birds, owls, and bats are also friendly pest controllers. Put up a birdhouse or bat box to attract them.

✓ Create your own organic anti-insect potion with garlic, peppers, borax, or soap.

✓ Protect plants from deer and rabbits with fences made of garden mesh, which is inexpensive and unobtrusive.

✓ Apply mulch, covering the soil with straw, grass clippings, bark chips, or leaves. This discourages weeds, keeps the soil moist, moderates temperature swings, and ultimately decomposes to add enrichment to the soil.

Getting help

You don't have to do it alone. The new career of gardening coach exists to help people get started, make choices, and have their questions answered. "We try to teach people how to do it themselves, not do it for them," says Susan Harris, a coach in Maryland. The nationwide healthy grocery chain Whole Foods has a gardening coach, too. On the other hand, some itinerant gardeners *will* do it for you. If you live in Portland, Oregon, you can hire Your Backyard Farmer to plant a vegetable garden on your land and do the cultivating and harvesting. Similar projects are springing up in other cities, as urban agriculture grows. Journalist Kim Severson calls this "remote-controlled backyard gardening."

Veggies in the city

New Roots Urban Farm was founded in St. Louis by three friends who got a state grant to buy six city-owned abandoned lots. The money collected from shareholders went for seeds and tools. Soil and compost were donated. Today New Roots has many shareholders and also sells produce at a farmers' market. Best of all, the urban farm gives neighborhood kids the chance to tend the crops and then cook what they've grown.

Fringe benefits

Besides cooking and eating your produce, you can also give it to food banks or swap it with friends and neighbors for their produce, creating your own mini-economy. Or you can sell it—some restaurants buy from local mini-farmers. To make the most of a surplus when your crops ripen, you could revive the venerable kitchen arts of preserving and canning.

What you can do:
- ✓ Start with something that's likely to succeed. You can buy kits with pots, soil, instructions, and already planted seeds. As you gain experience, branch out.
- ✓ Get seeds from a garden or hardware store, by mail order, or online.
- ✓ Contact a seed preservation group and plant some heirloom varieties.
- ✓ Practice growing food by volunteering at a community supported farm.
- ✓ Find your local community gardening group, where citizens join together to plant and tend gardens. Some food co-ops have a garden as one of their programs.
- ✓ Install bee blocks that solitary wild bees can use.
- ✓ Stop using pesticides around the house.
- ✓ If your community doesn't have a gardening group, start one.

If you perceive gardening as work, it will seem like work, making it harder to persevere until you see the payoffs. But if you see gardening as a labor of love, an alternative to the stationary bikes at the athletic club, a spiritual re-connection to the productive cycles of our Earth, and an opportunity to heal a little patch of land, it is a success by any measure.

—Science teacher and avid gardener,
    Andy Snow

Answer to question from page 14.

Of all the actions you can take to make your food style earth-friendly, the one with the greatest number of advantages is *growing your own food.* You can:

Guarantee that your food is organic
Preserve heritage varieties
Create less waste
Use your own compost
Eat food that tastes better
Save money
Use no packaging or refrigerated transport
Get fresh air and exercise, and
Offer your produce as a wonderful gift.

Nurture capital--the other kind of growing

Slow Money, a new non-profit organization, funnels investment dollars to small food enterprises and local food systems. The Slow Money philosophy is, "Soil fertility, carrying capacity, sense of place, care of the commons, cultural, ecological and economic health and diversity, nonviolence–these are the fundamentals of nurture capital, a new financial sector supporting the emergence of a restorative economy." This is just what we need for the new food world! I also like their motto: "In Soil We Trust."

Spice Up Your Social Life

How many times have you heard the lament that modern fast-paced life leaves little time for community? That we are isolated and don't know our neighbors? The new world of Earth-friendly eating can help fill the gap.

The organization Slow Food is a conscious revolt against everything fast food stands for. Slow Food means good quality food shared at a leisurely pace, with time and respect given to mealtime with family and friends. Slow Food means diverse varieties of healthful foods grown locally and prepared lovingly, and the sustaining of small, artisanal producers, such as local cheese makers and wine producers. There are over 83,000 members in 122 countries. Leaders of Slow Food promote local food artisans and organize events such as wine tastings and visits to farmers' markets.

Though there are many wonderful vegetarian restaurants, in many other restaurants vegetarians are lucky to find a single entrée they can eat, usually some tired version of pasta. At national and local vegetarian organizations, members get together for meals, activism, and social occasions.

Gardeners, whose avocation represents the largest single hobby in America, form local clubs to exchange ideas and encouragement. The National Gardening Association offers resources, brings gardening to schools, and builds community gardening groups.

Members of buying cooperatives save money and time by buying wholesale and sharing the costs. These are small local word-of-mouth groups, so if you don't belong to one and you like the idea, start one. At cooking classes, you can learn about ethnic cooking and other unfamiliar foods and meet people in your neighborhood.

And don't forget Community Supported Agriculture, the farms you can join as a subscriber. If your CSA leaves its weekly shipments at a drop-off point, you may run into friends and neighbors on your pickup day. Some CSA farms also hold harvest festivals and other celebratory events. If you grow food, why not try holding a harvest party or canning bee?

Underground food economy

Iso Rabins is a San Francisco urban forager, gathering wild mushrooms, greens, and acorns. Since his work didn't fit into the categories required by food safety rules, he held "underground markets" in people's homes. Rabins calls the system a club for buyers and an incubator for other food entrepreneurs. At a recent invitation-only market, homemade jams, butter, and beef jerky were among the products offered by dozens of sellers. Forewarned buyers know these products are not produced by inspected kitchens, and take responsibility for their own safety while forming a market for small-scale food artisans. Food inspection (especially of huge corporate operations) has a vital role in our food world, and so does the spirit of entrepreneurship and personal responsibility.

PART V

PART V
Food for Thought

Why do people disagree over environmental issues? At one extreme, some people deny or minimize the problems, perhaps hoping the fuss will go away, or perhaps having a vested interest in the way things are now. At the other extreme, passionate environmentalists sometimes criticize existing solutions because they can imagine even better ones. We need a way to navigate these important debates.

These are my guidelines:

If experts think there is a danger but they don't agree on its exact extent, I recommend the precautionary principle: Better safe than sorry.

If ingenious and dedicated people have devised good solutions that may not be perfect, I say: Better some progress now than waiting for perfection later.

> Most of the things worth doing in the world had been declared impossible before they were done.
>
> —United States Supreme Court Justice
> Louis Brandeis

Dueling Data: Trade-offs and the Learning Curve

Environmental issues are complex. Scientists discover new interrelationships in nature. An invention may solve one problem but create another one. A discovery or recommendation made sincerely by one researcher or activist may be criticized just as sincerely by another. There are changing cultural trends, new products, new technologies, new lists of endangered species—it's impossible to know everything.

I see four main reasons for confusion and disagreement about environmental solutions.

First, **nature is vast and complicated**. Scientists are still working out the complex webs of each ecosystem, and there are hundreds of ecosystems. The web of damage we have done is as complex as the web of life. That's why ecologists may criticize each other—they see different aspects of the torn web and know that one repair will not fix the whole.

Second, actions taken with good intentions may lead to undesirable outcomes. A solution in one generation (such as the invention of pesticides) becomes a problem in the next (pollution of soil and water, and harm to our bodies). This is the **law of unintended consequences**.

Third, there's a range of perspectives and response styles with **different time frames**. Some people respond to emergencies, while others engage in long-range planning.

Finally, **some solutions require trade-offs.** We'll need to refine our skill in balancing competing interests and learn to live with imperfect answers.

Tradeoffs

Trade-offs occur when good intentions compete against hard realities or against other good intentions. For example, to alleviate poverty in Africa, high-producing Holstein cows were imported, which can produce 20 times as much milk as the local breed. But Holsteins are costly to maintain and crowd out indigenous cattle. Ankole cattle in Uganda, indigenous pigs in Viet Nam, and native sheep in Kenya are endangered in this way, reducing biodiversity.

In this country, take biofuels—fuels made from corn or palm oil. They could bring independence from oil imports, but they divert land and crops away from food supplies and can actually hurt the environment: Palm-based agrofuel might generate ten times more carbon dioxide per gallon than gasoline. Land to grow palm would be cleared by cutting down rainforests, which are already in danger and which are vital for biodiversity and carbon sequestration. To top it off, the United Nations predicts that as many as 5 million people would be displaced from their lands. So should we adopt biofuels?

Trade-offs can also occur as a side-effect of success. Organic farming has had phenomenal growth in market share. Should organic growers borrow big business practices in order to reach even more people—or does that mean they are selling out? What if organic companies are bought by big corporations–can they maintain their standards?

The man in between

David Mas Masumoto grows organic peaches and grapes. In a recent article (humorously entitled "Married to Walmart: What Was I Thinking?"), he described his mixed feelings about selling his fruit to the retail giant. He wondered, "Was Walmart, the slick city suitor, trying to sweep us naive country folks off our feet then suck the life out of us? Or was I an idealistic organic farmer, believing I could help hundreds of acres transition to organic, reduce pesticide use and protect the health of farmers and farm workers?" Some of his organic friends gave mixed reactions to his Walmart partnership, but Masumoto has also met conventional farmers who are getting ready to go organic. The transition continues. Every farmer and every consumer has a story to tell.

Many innovations involve such trade-offs or go through a stage of criticism and debate. That's to be expected. When you read in the news that a certain good idea has critics, don't be surprised—just stay tuned, watching out for greenwash and deceptive public relations.

Another response to complex issues is to choose the least harmful option. You don't have time to investigate every consumer issue, but you can adopt the precautionary principle: better safe than sorry. For example, it's probably wise to limit your exposure to the thousands of toxic chemicals that have not been fully tested for human safety.

The learning curve

Some environmental problems occur because not enough was known when a solution was first tried. For instance, to reduce over-fishing in the Gulf of Mexico, limits were set: shorter legal fishing seasons and limits on the size of fish that could be caught. But these rules backfired. To make the most of the shorter season, fishers built bigger boats. To get around catch limits, they threw back dead or dying smaller fish so they could then catch bigger ones. A new program allots a part of the overall catch to each fisher as a secure fishing privilege, benefiting both fish and fishers. I suspect that flaws will eventually be found in this new system, too, and then another round of improvements will be needed.

Decisions, decisions. What happens when a corporation that has been a polluter or exploiter starts to improve its environmental record? How do you know if it has changed enough that you can now in good conscience patronize it? You can't monitor every issue and every business, but you can try to keep informed and make sustainable choices. You can read labels and learn which watchdog organizations to trust. You can be willing to seek up-to-date information and adjust your purchases accordingly.

You be the judge

Here are two proposed solutions to our food-related environment problems. Do they help or harm? This is your chance to practice balancing tradeoffs.

> Flexible food-wrapping film can now be made from crops (corn, sugarcane, sweet potatoes). This could help us reduce the amount of petroleum that we turn into plastic; these new materials are also biodegradable. But bioplastics divert food crops, require land and water, and release carbon dioxide in the manufacturing process.

> Soybeans are lower on the food chain than beef, causing less environmental damage. But most soybeans are now genetically modified and require more pesticides and herbicides. Also, soybeans are grown overseas in lands that have been cleared of rainforest, which is urgently needed for biodiversity and carbon sequestration.

Balance hope and caution

The biggest danger (apart from total denial) is that we will be lulled into thinking that "someone" has solved the problem (or will solve it soon) and that we as individuals don't have to do anything. This is false optimism. A second danger is what I call "graywash," being too discouraged, not giving enough credit to those working to save the environment, not allowing ourselves to hope or to take the many little steps we can take each day. This is false pessimism.

In fact, each one of us can help our environment by taking the steps we believe in, learning about additional choices, and remembering that our daily actions impact the web of life.

What you can do:

✓ Learn about both sides of a debate.
✓ Be alert for greenwash (ploys to exploit your idealism) and graywash (too much cynicism).
✓ Identify labels and watchdog groups you trust.
✓ Reduce or eliminate consumption of products that you have doubts about.
✓ Respect honest efforts to be sustainable, though they may not be perfect.

Help Endangered Species

The phrase "endangered species" usually makes us think of pandas, whales, and mountain gorillas. But thousands of other species are also endangered—over 41,000 species worldwide.

We are causing extinctions of species by destroying their habitats to build cities, or by stripping soil for mining and factories, or by poisoning their habitats, or by disrupting their food supply, or by interfering with their life cycle with our pollution, light, and noise. Many people think that animals and natural places have a right to exist, just as humans do. Furthermore, indigenous people may need the threatened plants and animals.

There are other impacts: if one part of an ecosystem goes, the whole web could unravel; plants that could provide future medicines or substances could be lost; and genetic diversity is reduced. Without genetic diversity, one blight could kill an entire crop (as happened in Ireland in the nineteenth century, when a potato blight caused the starvation of millions of people) and inbreeding can occur (which creates health problems in animals and humans).

The damage we do in one place or niche travels along the web of life to do damage elsewhere. For example, farming and ranching runoff (which includes nitrogen and phosphorous) contributes to algae blooms, which helps snail populations increase, which spurs parasites that deform frogs. When a species disappears, a whole food web can collapse or deteriorate.

There are signs of hope. The Renewing America's Food Traditions collaborative (RAFT) lists over a thousand threatened food plants and animals unique to North America, including the Seminole pumpkin, white paypop passionfruit, Sonoran white pomegranate, and Pueblo red dye amaranth. Paradoxically, sometimes the best thing we can do to preserve a species is to add it to our diets. Slow Food, the group

125

that rebels against industrial food and hasty eating, promotes "eater-based conservation" and has created the Ark of Taste. This designation encourages chefs, grocers, educators, and consumers to sustain endangered food varieties.

You can help three kinds of endangered species with your food choices: domestic, imported, and sea life. Sometimes this means eating more of them, and sometimes it means eating less or none.

Domestic

By eating more heritage apples, quinoa, spelt flour, quince and many other varieties of fruits, vegetables, and grains, you encourage people to grow and sell them. You might even consider growing some of these rare species in your own garden. This is also true of farmed animals. The American Livestock Breeds Conservancy (ALBC) works to preserve over 150 threatened breeds of livestock—cattle, goats, horses, sheep, pigs, rabbits, chickens, ducks, geese, and turkeys. ALBC conducts research, maintains gene banks, rescues threatened populations, educates people about genetic diversity, and offers technical support to breeders, associations, and farmers. Small farms around the country raise Jacob sheep, Buckeye chickens, Jersey Buff turkeys, and many more.

Imported

Palm oil production is one of the main causes of rainforest destruction, according to the Rainforest Action Network. Other foods (beef and soy) are also grown on land that was once rainforest. Try to avoid palm oil, and buy organic U.S.-grown soy. Buy banana, coffee, and chocolate only if they are organic and fair trade. Not all of these foods are endangered, but growing them in industrial ways can endanger the lands they come from.

Sea life

What surprised me most when I researched this book was how much sea life is threatened by human fishing. Not just whales and dolphins, but also fish of many kinds are sinking in numbers, as are mollusks (such as squids) and crustaceans (such as lobsters). So my overall recommendation is that you eat less fish, octopus, lobster, and other sea life—or none. Environmental facts are constantly changing, partly due to worsening conditions, but sometimes due to successes. Still, we need to be vigilant: while some species have been taken off the endangered species list, others have been added. Vote with your fork to keep the successes coming.

What you can do:

- ✓ Keep up to date on what sea life is endangered, and don't eat it. Tell restaurants why you are avoiding endangered fish.
- ✓ Encourage restaurants and caterers to join the Chefs Collaborative.
- ✓ Try vegetarian dishes.
- ✓ At your grocery or farmers' market, buy unusual fruits and vegetables.
- ✓ Grow some food, choosing heirloom or heritage varieties.
- ✓ Buy unusual foods from an ethnic grocery or CSA (Community Supported Agriculture farm).

All creatures near and far

To save endangered species, Oakland Zoo in California supports over a dozen projects around the world, including Chimp Haven, The Sun Bear Project, Save the Tigers, the Bushmeat Crisis Task Force, Budongo Snare Removal Project, and Amigos de las Aves. On site, the zoo recycles and uses environmentally safe products in the café, including biodegradable plates and utensils made of cornstarch. The zoo uses leftover grease as biodiesel fuel in its maintenance vehicles. The Zoomobile, which takes small ambassador animals to schools, is a Prius. The zoo has participated in creek restoration, planted native (drought-tolerant) plants, and installed solar panels in its education building. Its Earth Day event draws over 4,000 visitors to its speaker events and educational programs. Oakland Zoo is not the only one taking such actions—the American Zoo Association requires that its 221 member zoos support conservation projects around the world.

Animal Farm

You may assume that the cows, pigs, and chickens destined for our tables live decent lives in farms regulated by somebody and that they are subjected to a quick and painless death. Sad to say, it's not true. Billions of cows, chickens, and pigs live their entire lives in appalling conditions in factory farms (Confined Animal Feeding Operations, CAFOs) owned or controlled by large corporations. Farm animals are not protected by any federal laws on the farm, and most states exempt "customary" agricultural practices from their statutes against cruelty to animals.

Some good news

The market for cage-free eggs is growing in grocery stores, 400 Bon Appetit outlets, and 150 college and university food services. A growing number of ranchers let animals eat grass and roam outside (of course, there have always been some people who did so). Pastured (grass-fed) cattle are not given the corn diet that uses up the corn harvest. (Recall that eating corn also gives the cows digestive disorders, for which CAFO operators give them antibiotics). Pastured chickens get real access to outdoors, with outdoor pens that are rotated around the fields to prevent saturation of the soil with their droppings and to allow them access to new land.

In the American Humane Certified program, farm animals are raised in cage-free environments that limit stress and prevent injury and disease; have access to prompt medical care if problems do occur; have ready access to fresh water and a healthful diet; are free to express their natural behaviors; and live in "an appropriate and comfortable environment that includes sufficient space, proper facilities, shelter, a resting area, and company of the animals' own kind." One such farm in Louisiana is the family-owned Kleinpeter Farms. Managing over 600 cows on 1,500 acres, the farmers received the 2007 Louisiana Wildlife Federation Conservation award for setting an example of environmentally progressive agriculture. The Kleinpeter farm produces

129

dairy products, but doesn't use hormones to force growth and milk production.

If you eat meat, help create a market for humane treatment of animals. For a few pennies more per pound, you can buy organic or humanely certified meat and help end the cycle of cruelty.

What you can do:
- ✓ If you eat meat, buy USDA organic or American Humane Certified.
- ✓ Write to your elected representatives protesting cruelty on factory farms.
- ✓ Visit United Poultry Concerns at upc-online.org to learn about alternatives to cruelty to chickens, ducks, and turkeys.
- ✓ If you sincerely want to improve the lot of animals, you could eat less of them—or none at all.

The Nutrition-Industrial Complex

Americans eat well on a smaller share of their incomes than most other countries—11% on average. Industrial agriculture makes possible this affordable food marketplace. Planting thousands of acres of the same crop makes it easier to harvest and market. Merging the slaughter plants creates efficiency. Building thousands of identical mega-stores makes selling more profitable. Food is big business—a $1 trillion sector of the American economy—but food production has become concentrated into fewer and fewer hands.

- Four meatpacking firms control 84% of the U.S. slaughtering industry, and eight firms control two thirds of the poultry business.
- One wholesale company, Houston-based Sysco, supplies food to 400,000 eating establishments, from fast-food chains to fancy restaurants, offering everything from bags of rice to elegant desserts.

Big Food fights regulations, undermines organic labeling, hires public relations firms to spread "manufactured uncertainty," pays schools to sell junk food and beverages, and contributes heavily to politicians in order to defend the industrialized food economy.

> We are managing our planet as if it were a business in liquidation.
>
> —Wisconsin Senator and Earth Day founder Gaylord Nelson.

Food safety

Contamination hits the headlines every few years when an outbreak or new illness claims human lives. But the causes of contamination are always there: underfunded and scattered government agencies, the profit motive that encourages producers to cut corners, overcentralization, and industry opposition to regulation. For example, the food industry successfully avoided the introduction of paper and electronic records. As a result, during the salmonella outbreak of 2008 it took so long for regulators to track down the cause that many extra poisoning cases occurred. Instead of cleaning up slaughtering plants, industry uses irradiation, antibiotics and even dipping animal carcasses in disinfectants to mitigate contamination after it's already occurred. Dr. David Kessler, former commissioner of the FDA, said bluntly, "Our food safety system is broken." As of this writing, a food safety bill has just been signed into law. Let us hope that it is properly funded and enforced.

Advertising and public relations

America's food industry (including beverage, supplements, and food service) spends $30 billion a year to advertise its products. Processed foods bring the greatest profit, so the most heavily advertised foods are things like frozen pizzas, children's cereals, convenience foods, candy, and snacks, which tend to be the least healthy and to contribute to obesity.

Children are coveted targets. Food corporations spend $1.6 billion a year to advertise food to children, skillfully manipulating them to gain what they call "share of mind" and "life-time brand loyalty" by "viral marketing" and inculcating in children "the nag factor," "pester power," and "the fine art of whining." Whenever bad news about a product or industry hits the front pages, public relations professionals hired by the industry step up to soothe concerns, to delay and dilute action. Their goal is to make it appear that the critics are biased, or exaggerating the problem, or plain wrong. One PR professional admitted, "Our product is doubt." They've even succeeded in creating doubt about climate change. A national columnist commented,

The denial machine is running at full throttle—and continuing to shape both government policy and public opinion. Since the late 1980s, this well-coordinated, well-funded campaign by contrarian scientists, free-market think tanks and industry has created a paralyzing fog of doubt around climate change.

—Sharon Begley in *Newsweek*

PR hired guns are all too effective—they kept tobacco, a known killer, out of regulators' power for over four decades, and are now using the same tactics to protect the food industry. For instance, when the Environmental Working Group published a list of the fruits and vegetables most likely to contain pesticide residues, an industry group attacked the list as "an impediment to public health."

Lobbying and co-opting legislators

Though it's not in our Constitution, we have a de facto fourth branch of government: lobbies, interest groups that hire professionals to influence legislators. This is not necessarily a bad thing—many of us belong to professions or organizations that hire lobbyists to persuade legislators. The meat industry has lobbyists, as do sugar, wheat, fishers, and the rest.

But these lobbyists are paid to protect the industry, not consumers. When the Country-of-Origin Label law was passed in 2002, meat importers and grocery retailers blocked it from being enforced. The Department of Labor conveniently changed laws about reporting workplace injuries, making it appear that slaughter plants are safe.

Campaign donations accomplish the same goal of protecting their interests at the expense of the public. Even if a law to improve food safety gets passed, industry doesn't give up—it just weakens the regulatory agency by making sure it doesn't have enough funding or enough clout. Tactics include wining and dining legislators and regulators, and offering them high-paying jobs. This tempts them to leave government for corporate positions, in the famous "revolving door."

Externalizing costs

Many industries, including agriculture, can sell their products relatively cheaply because they don't pay the full cost of manufacturing them. They "externalize" costs by simply ignoring the health or environmental impacts of their work. So taxpayers pay for cleaning up environmental damage; patients and insurance companies pay for medical treatments. This is one reason organic and more humanely grown foods appear more expensive—the conventional growers simply shift part of their expenses onto us.

Business can be green—they've proved it

Patagonia, manufacturer of outdoor clothing and gear, donates 1% of sales to environmental groups, $31 million so far. Patagonia uses only organic cotton—significant because cotton is one of the most pesticide-intensive products sold. Patagonia also uses wind and solar power, adopts green building practices, heats its plants by recirculating hot water, and uses motion detectors to reduce light use. Patagonia works to reduce its manufacturing footprint and makes its supply path transparent on its web site. It founded The Conservation Alliance in 1989 to encourage other outdoor companies to support environmental organizations. No wonder that betterworldshopper.org voted Patagonia the #2 Best Company on the Planet.

Undermining free speech

The most outrageous activity agribusiness uses to defend its ways is to attack our most precious civil liberty—freedom of speech. Oprah Winfrey and her guest, former cattle rancher Howard Lyman, were sued by cattlemen for their televised comments about beef. In 2005, the Sugar Association threatened to sue a cable television network that ran anti-sugar ads on children's shows. A fast food chain hired infiltrators to spy on college students who were supporting farm workers' rights.

"Food disparagement laws" have been passed in 13 states, making it easier for food producers to sue their critics. Nutrition expert Marion Nestle (no relation to the food corporation) has revealed, in her book *Food Politics*, how the food industry successfully suppressed government attempts to offer the simple, sane advice, "eat less." It took years of legal action to win Ohio dairy farmers the right to label their milk as hormone-free.

But the industry does demand freedom of speech for itself. Public health attorney Michele Simon, in her book *Appetite for Profit*, describes how the food industry uses "free speech" arguments to defend manipulative advertising of junk food to children. (She also offers a hilarious anti-glossary of corporate spin words).

Patenting life

Chemical manufacturers, wanting to retain their market for pesticides, invented crops they can patent by modifying their genes so the plants can survive massive doses of pesticides. Some farmers do not want to plant such crops—but if patented pollen from a neighboring farm drifts onto their fields, their own crops are then contaminated with genetically modified seeds. The scariest single thing I found when researching this book: manufacturers can then sue those farmers for patent infringement. Patenting seeds, the very source of life, takes away the last resort of those who want some control over what they put into their bodies.

Why do they do all this?

Are the people who make these decisions all greedy and evil? Psychologists, including researcher Philip Zimbardo, have found disquieting evidence that any person, in certain situations, can do evil deeds. What is the situation in which agribusiness executives operate? They're competing with each other; they're under pressure to keep food prices low; industrializing has made food production seem efficient; and they inherited a tempting golden goose of federal subsidies. And don't underestimate the power of the attitude, "Everyone's doing it."

Even larger than any given Situation is the System, Zimbardo points out. The System here is our investment philosophy that an industry must keep growing and show profits in the short term. People we don't even associate with food, Wall Street analysts, predict how much a corporation "should" earn, and woe to the company (and the CEO) that falls short of the prediction—even if it actually made a profit. Making costly changes that help the Earth doesn't look good on quarterly profit-and-loss statements.

Our System also includes the government, with lobbying, campaign donations, and the famous revolving door. Our System also includes deeply embedded values, such as our national pride in inventiveness, our identity as being at the top of the food chain, and our belief in "mastering" nature. The System includes our habits of overeating and the hectic pace that creates a market for heavily processed "convenience" foods.

So the sources of the destructive activities of agribusiness reach far beyond executive offices. As I've shown you throughout this book, you can do something about this.

The positive side of big business

When business leaders decide to do the right thing, they can have enormous impact. When Walmart began selling organic food, buying more local produce, and requiring that its suppliers make environmentally responsible steps, thousands of companies had to change their ways if they wanted to sell their products to Walmart. When grocery chain Safeway established an organic house brand for 300 items in its 1,775 stores and 500 affiliates, the market for organic growers expanded and organic food was made easily available to many more people.

Ready for a surprise? Makower's Paradox. Sometimes corporations do the right thing—secretly. For example, Coke and Anheuser-Busch reduced the aluminum in their cans by almost a third without advertising the fact. The reason: Proclaiming a good step may call attention to a problem the public didn't even know existed, or risk accusations of greenwash if the company hasn't solved all its environmental problems. There may be progress going on in corporations that we don't know about. Shall we call it stealthwash?

Citizen power

There is hope for our food system. Determined groups and individuals have stopped some of industry's worst tactics and even turned some businesses around. It's not good to have a giant against you, but if you can get the giant on your side, you're in luck.

What you can do:

- ✓ Support the companies and policies that are Earth-friendly.
- ✓ When you do buy from big businesses, choose ones that are making the transition to sustainability (while watching out for greenwash).
- ✓ Support legislation that punishes bad corporate practices and supports good ones. Tell your elected representatives why you do.
- ✓ Identify watchdog groups that you trust, and read their newsletters.
- ✓ Be willing to spend more money for Earth-friendly food. If you are on a tight budget, see the section (below) on Time and Money.

Good Intentions

Our higher selves are involved in food and eating, as we take active responsibility for the health of ourselves and our planet, remember the spiritual meaning of food, and express concern for other people, animals, and the environment.

Food for the spirit

Throughout history, people have held harvest festivals to give thanks and recognize a transcendent hand in the harvest. By sharing food, we share survival and the care and skill with which the food has been grown and prepared. We link to the past by cooking traditional dishes. Even those who do not think of themselves as religious may have spiritual feelings, expressed in a love of nature, high ethical standards, caring for others, artistic creativity, or an inexpressible sense of being woven into the universe. Food for the spirit means that your whole self is nurtured—not only the body, but also the social self who needs human contact, the creative self who longs to be expressed, and the questing self who wonders about it all. Many religious groups are taking an active part in restoring a sense of respect for the Earth, as are many non-religious people. Gratitude, stewardship, and responsibility are values you can honor with your food choices, whatever your worldview may be.

What you can do:

- ✓ Choose one holiday a year to practice good Earth stewardship.
- ✓ Join or initiate environmental awareness and action at your church, temple, mosque, or ashram.
- ✓ Share your bounty.
- ✓ Volunteer to serve at a homeless shelter.
- ✓ Get some exercise on food-centered holidays by going outside and cleaning up a local park or creek.

Fair trade

The people who grow our food, like people who make our clothes, toys, and furniture, are often exploited and underpaid, whether they live in this country or overseas. Fortunately, caring individuals and organizations are creating ways to ensure that the workers are justly compensated. In 2006, consumers spent over $2 billion on certified fair trade products, an increase of 42% in just one year. 3% of coffee sold in U.S. in 2006 was fair trade—more than eight times the level five of years earlier. Starbucks, McDonald's, and Sam's Club are starting to offer some fair trade products. Growing crops organically can even help fight poverty, since poor nations then spend less on expensive chemicals, get higher prices, and grow more diverse crops, helping preserve their soil. In Minnesota, Native Americans (Ojibwa) gather genuine wild rice. The White Earth Land Recovery Project preserves the harvest and makes sure the tribe gets a fair share of the proceeds.

What you can do:

✓ Look for "Fair Trade" coffee, cocoa, sugar, tea, bananas, honey, wine, and fresh fruit.

✓ Be willing to spend more for fair trade products. It's only fair.

Sweet success

Cacao growers in Ecuador were getting 20 cents a pound for their cacao beans. American Judy Logback helped them bypass the middleman and drove them 250 miles to the port, where they got 48 cents a pound. She also helped them build a cooperative of 850 families and hired an expert to help them learn to process the beans. They now get $1.95 a pound, giving them a fair return on their labor.

Vegetarianism

People choose a vegetarian lifestyle for various reasons: health, compassion for animals, concern about the meat industry's heavy burden on the environment, concern about people going hungry when so many resources go into making meat. A vegetarian does not eat animal flesh but does eat dairy and eggs. A vegan does not eat dairy or eggs, either.

Those unfamiliar with nutrition may worry that the vegetarian or vegan is not getting enough protein. In fact, protein exists in many plant foods, especially legumes, beans, and nuts; furthermore, humans do not need vast amounts of protein to be healthy. You can get all the protein you need from plant sources. Calcium and other nutrients are present in plant-based diets. Medical research has repeatedly shown that vegetarians are often the most healthy people studied.

> It is the position of the American Dietetic Association that appropriately planned vegetarian diets (including total vegetarian or vegan diets) are healthful, nutritionally adequate, and may provide health benefits in the prevention and treatment of certain diseases.
>
> —American Dietetic Association

It is possible for a person to eat unhealthily as a vegetarian, just as a meat eater can eat unhealthily. Children or pre-teens may begin a vegetarian diet without the knowledge to choose the variety of foods necessary for health. A nutritionist knowledgeable about eating problems and about vegetarian options can help a person choose a healthy and satisfying diet.

What you can do:

- ✓ Realize that vegetarianism is usually a safe lifestyle chosen thoughtfully. Offer acceptance to your vegetarian friends, relatives, and co-workers.
- ✓ Learn some vegetarian recipes and include meat-free dishes when you entertain.
- ✓ Try some meat-free entrees when you dine out, encouraging the restaurant to offer these choices.
- ✓ Consider adopting a vegetarian way of life.

Eating lightly for the Earth

Overeating is part of the environmental crisis. We are eating larger portions and consuming several hundred more calories a day than we did in the 1950s. Our food system supplies 3,800 calories a day for every man, woman, and child. Though some is wasted, this is far more food than we need. And it isn't even making us healthy. World Watch Institute says, "As caloric-rich junk foods squeeze healthy items from the diet, obesity often masks nutrient starvation. [People are] essentially trading diseases of dietary deficiency for diseases of dietary excess."

Unless we change our ways, almost 90% of Americans will be overweight or obese by 2030. Much of the obesity problem is caused by our sedentary lifestyle and other factors (such as genes, age, and metabolism). Still, many of us could do very well on less than we're consuming. Why do we eat so much? Partly we've forgotten how much food we actually need. We're surrounded by treats of all kinds, prepared temptingly and sold conveniently. Another reason is emotional. Some people use food as an anesthetic, reward, punisher, and procrastination device. Others overeat because they are depressed, self-medicating with comfort food.

Meanwhile, food scientists study the precise proportions of sugar, fat, and salt that are biologically the most appealing to the human animal, and use this knowledge to manufacture food products such as candy and potato chips that are especially hard to resist. (This is another reason to focus your food dollars on fresh local foods). Recall that food manufacturers spend billions of dollars to advertise processed food and more dollars to hobble government regulators. You are the target of these efforts. If you overeat their products, it's not entirely your fault.

One final reason we may be overeating is that food from animals—meat, dairy, and eggs—is very calorie-dense. To fill our stomachs, we may consume more meat and dairy calories than if we were eating fresh fruits and vegetables.

So eating less, eating lightly for the Earth, helps both you and your fellow creatures. Eating with the Earth in mind means thinking about others: animals, water, air, soil, and present and future generations of people. Is the farmer who grew my vegetables prospering? Is the worker who picked my strawberries made ill by the pesticides she is exposed to in the fields? What happened to the prairie animals when the wheat fields were planted? Is this hamburger hurting the rain forest?

Uh oh. Is this going to be a guilt trip?

No, no, a thousand times no. Guilt doesn't work. Guilt makes us want to avoid the whole topic, forget the problems, and go have a steak. I'm proposing the opposite: getting excited about food choices that are healthy for you and the planet, feeling a calm self-respecting desire to be a good force in the world, and choosing food and other things to live in harmony with the Earth.

Time and Money

You may be thinking, "How can I afford to save the Earth? Who has the time or money?" Here are food choices you can make, depending on whether you have more time, more money, or not enough of either.

You have more time than money

- Cook at home rather than eating at restaurants or buying convenience foods.
- Brown bag your meals at work, school, or volunteer activities.
- Grow your own food in pots or in your yard.
- Join a community garden and grow some food.
- Use leftovers.
- Compost the scraps.
- Volunteer at an environmental organization.
- Avoid excess packaging by buying foods in bulk.
- Eat less meat, dairy, and fish—or none.

You have more money than time

- Buy organic foods.
- Join a Community Supported Agriculture farm.
- If you buy prepared and frozen foods, choose vegetarian ones.
- Patronize green restaurants.
- Tell other restaurants to go green—and hand the owners and managers a copy of this book.
- Avoid excess packaging.
- Share extras with local food banks.

Broke and busy—not enough time or money

- Learn one good soup or stew recipe for using leftovers.
- Eat less meat, dairy, and fish—or none.
- Buy from Earth-friendly producers.
- Practice these suggestions one at a time.
- Spread the knowledge in this book to friends, family, coworkers, and members of your community.

Small changes in our lives, multiplied by thousands, add up to a revolution. We can't wait for radical conservation measures to be imposed on us by our government—that takes a courage that our political system probably can never muster, no matter who's in charge. The way to look at it, I think, is that WE are in charge, individually and collectively. By proving to myself that my family can learn to live well with less, drastically reducing our foodmiles and our carbon footprint, I'm giving myself the courage to require more responsibility from myself, my fellow citizens, and our government.

—Barbara Kingsolver, author of
Animal, Vegetable, Miracle

The Win-Win-Win Situation

Everyone wins if we eat with the Earth in mind. People living today will be healthier, our children will inherit a more livable planet, and animals and ecosystems gain a chance to recover. We can take personal responsibility for tackling global warming. We can help save family farms and build community.

The producers of food (both small farms and forward-looking agricultural interests) are developing Earth-friendly methods of growing your food. Distributors (regional alliances of growers, health food stores, and increasingly, large supermarket chains) are making it available. Now it is up to you, the consumer, to encourage them by buying what they have produced with the Earth in mind.

Ask yourself, "What kind of world do I want? What can I do with my food choices to help the Earth?" Then act in order to bring it about. If you want a world that has clean air, streams running free, healthy humans, open space for wild animals, and topsoil that will feed our great-grandchildren, then you can help build this world by making Earth-friendly food choices.

> All over the world there are people who have entered into the exercise of imagining a sustainable world. They can see it as a world to move toward, not reluctantly, not with a sense of sacrifice or regret, but joyfully. It could be a very much better world than the one we live in today.
>
> —Donella Meadows, Dennis Meadows, and Jorgen Randers, authors of *The Limits to Growth.*

Web Sites and Organizations

Hundreds of organizations in North America are working to green our collective foodprint. Here are some of my favorites.

- appetiteforprofit.com. Exposes questionable practices of agribusiness.
- betterworldshopper.org. Grades corporations, including food producers, on their environmental impact, human rights, and other issues.
- chefscollaborative.org. Nationwide group of food professionals who support sustainable agriculture and help chefs transition to Earth-friendly practices.
- earthsave.org. National organization for the health of person and planet, offering education and support for choosing a plant-based diet for over 20 years.
- eatwellguide.org. A free online directory of local sustainable food, with thousands of listings—farms, markets, restaurants, CSAs, and more.
- fishphone.org. Can be accessed from mobile devices so you can choose fish with the Earth in mind. Blueocean.org/seafood.org, the computer site related to fishphone, is a nonprofit consumer group that advocates safe food produced sustainably and humanely.
- foodandwaterwatch.org. Advocates for policies that support safe and sustainable food and water, and offers informative newsletters.
- foodpolitics.com. Consumer defender and food expert Marion Nestle's ongoing watchdog site.
- greenerchoices.org/eco-labels. From Consumers Union (which produces Consumer Reports), this site helps you decide if an eco-label is genuine and meaningful.
- hsus.org. The Humane Society of the United States conducts research and campaigns to change the cruel factory farm system.

- localharvest.org. Powerful search engine for finding organic and local food nationwide at Community Supported Agriculture farms and farmers' markets.
- msc.org. The Marine Stewardship Council labels sustainable seafood and educates consumers, producers, and fisheries worldwide.
- organicconsumers.org. Gives information about campaigns for organic, fair trade, honest labeling, food safety, health, and more.
- slowmoney.org. Creates investment funds to support local sustainable food systems.
- ucsusa.org/food_and_agriculture. Union of Concerned Scientists reports explain the science of agriculture and give practical tools to help consumers shop wisely.
- whatsonmyfood.org. From Pesticide Action Network, this site tells you what carcinogens, endocrine disruptors, neurotoxins, and other chemicals are found in foods.

SaveNature.org, my non-profit partner, raises money to save rainforest and coral reefs while educating children and adults about the importance of saving habitats and species. Edible EdVentures is our food and environment project. All author's profits from this book go to these programs.

Visit thegreenfoodprint.com for more information.

Sources

Our food world is changing rapidly, with many positive developments and many sources of information. I consulted scholarly journals, books by experts, daily journalism, business and technology journals and magazines, United States government and United Nations reports, and environmental nonprofit group reports and newsletters. On some issues, I made personal contact with experts. Please note: web addresses were accurate at the time of printing.

Preface

$1 trillion: Economic Research Service of the USDA, "Food CPI and Expenditures," August 25, 2010, www.ers.usda.gov/Briefing/CPIFoodAndExpenditures.

$2,577: Calculated from Bureau of Labor Statistics, Economic News Release, "Consumer Expenditures 2009," October 5, 2010, www.bls.gov/news.release/cesan.nr0.htm

"Daily voting booth": Paul Hawken, *The Ecology of Commerce: A Declaration of Sustainability* (New York: HarperBusiness, 1994), 212.

Introduction

"Like those big Industrial Age factories": Dan Barber, "Change We Can Stomach," *New York Times,* May 11, 2008.

How Can Food Be a Problem?

Dead zones: Robert J. Diaz and Rutger Rosenberg, "Spreading Dead Zones and Consequences for Marine Ecosystems," Science 321 (August 15, 2008): 926–929 [Abstract]. See also Scott C. Doney, "The Growing Human Footprint On Coastal and Open-Ocean Biogeochemistry," Science 328 (June 18, 2010): 1512–1516 [Abstract].

Rainforests cut down or burned: Rainforest Action Network, "New Report: Cargill Caught Destroying Rainforests, Endangering Orangutans," May 4, 2010, http://ran.org/content/new-report-cargill-caught-destroying-rainforests-endangering-orangutans. See also Rainforest Action Network, "The Problem with Palm Oil," September 22, 2010, www.ran.org /content/problem-palm-oil.

70% of previously forested land in the Amazon: Food and Agricultural Organization, *Livestock's Long Shadow* (United Nations, 2006), www.fao.org/docrep/010/a0701e/a0701e00.HTM . See also Humane Society of the United States, "The Impact of Animal Agriculture on Global Warming and Climate Change," 2008. See also Greenpeace, "United Plantations Certified Despite Gross Violations of RSPO Standards," 2008, www.greenpeace.org/usa/en/media-center/reports/united-plantations-certified-d.

Losing topsoil: Susan S. Lang, "'Slow, Insidious' Soil Erosion Threatens Human Health and Welfare, as Well as The Environment," *Cornell University Chronicle Online*, March 20, 2006, www.news.cornell.edu/stories/March06/soil.erosion.threat.ssl.html.

"The prospect of 5 billion people": Alan Durning, "The Fat of the Land," *World Watch Magazine,* July, 1992.

Monoculture: Union of Concerned Scientists, "Industrial Agriculture: Features and Policy," 2007, www.ucsusa.org/food_and_agriculture/science_and_impacts/impacts_industrial_agriculture/industrial-agriculture-features.html#Monoculture.

"All-you-can-eat restaurant for pests": quoted in Paul Hawken, Amory Lovins, and L. Hunter Lovins, *Natural Capitalism: Creating the Next Industrial Revolution* (Boston: Little, Brown, 1999), 195.

1,060 United States food species endangered: Gary Paul Nabhan, *Renewing America's Food Traditions* (White River Junction, VT: Chelsea Green, 2008), 3.

"Biodiversity—the sum total": Kenny Ausubel, *Restoring the Earth: Visionary Solutions from the Bioneers* (Tiburon, CA: H J Kramer, 1997), 42.

Organisms in a single field: Summarized from Vandana Shiva, *Stolen Harvest: The Hijacking of the Global Food Supply* (Cambridge, MA: South End Press, 2000), 61-62.

Bees dying: Josie Glasiusz, "Beepocalypse: Across the Country, Honeybees are Vanishing," *Discover*, June, 2007.

Almond trees: Gina Covina, "Nobody Home," *Terrain*, Summer 2007.

Destroying fragrance: "Study: Flowers Losing Smell," *Live Science*, April 11, 2008, www.livescience.com/environment/080411-pollution-flowers.html.

Virus-fungus combination: Kirk Johnson, "Scientists and Soldiers Solve a Bee Mystery," *New York Times*, October 7, 2010.

"Nature bats last": Paul Hawken, Amory Lovins, and L. Hunter Lovins, *Natural Capitalism: Creating the Next Industrial Revolution* (Boston: Little, Brown, 1999), 316.

Good News for the Earth

Thousands of non-profits: Paul Hawken, *Blessed Unrest* (New York: Viking, 2007). See the related website, www.wiserearth.org.

$3 trillion: "Socially Responsible Investing Facts," www.socialinvest.org/resources/sriguide/srifacts.cfm. In addition, institutional investors that represent $9 trillion in assets belong to the Investor Network on Climate Risk (www.incr.com).

20% per year: *Business Wire*, "Eating It Up: Organic Market Booms as Consumers Seek Healthier, More Natural Food and Drink Options," November 12, 2007. See also Carolyn Dimitri and Lydia Oberholtzer, "E.U. and U.S. Organic Markets Face Strong Demand Under Different Policies," USDA, February, 2006, www.ers.usda.gov/Amber-waves/February06/Features/Feature1.htm.

Over 6,000 farmers markets: USDA, Agricultural Marketing Service, "Farmers Markets and Local Food Marketing," www.ams.usda.gov/AMSv1.0/FARMERSMARKETS.

Conservation tilling: David Huggins and John Reganold, "No-Till: The Quiet Revolution," *Scientific American*, November, 2008.

1,667 land trusts: Hal Herring, "U.S. Land Trusts Make Huge Inroads: An Area Larger Than New England Now Protected," *Nature Conservancy Magazine*, Summer, 2007.

Blue Green Alliance: See www.bluegreenalliance.org.

8,000 cesspools: www.environmentaldefense.org, "Reform in the Heart of Hog Country," *Solutions* 38 (5) (2007): 7. See also Environmental Defense Fund's 2007 Annual Report, 13.

Environmental Defense and Frontline Farmers. "Cleaner Hog Farms in N.C. Could Be a National Model," *Solutions* 39 (4) (2008): 6, www.edf.org/documents/8225_Solutions_0808.pdf.

California Rangeland Conservation Coalition: "Campaign to Save California Range Unites Ranchers and Environmentalists," *Solutions* 38 (5) (2007): 6. See also www.ca-rangeland.org.

Fort Hood: Michele Amador Lopez and David Wolfe, "Cows, Tanks and Conservation: The Right Mix for Songbird Recovery," October 10, 2007, www.edf.org/article.cfm?contentID=7032.

U.S. Climate Action Partnership (USCAP): www.us-cap.org. See also Environmental Defense, "U.S. Climate Action Partnership Doubles, More CEOs Call for Cap on Carbon," May 8, 2007, www.edf.org/pressrelease.cfm?contentID=6348.

Turning off truck engines: "Wal-Mart Sees the Light," Environmental Defense Fund Annual Report 2007, 7. See also "Wal-Mart Steps Forward on Solar Power," *Solutions* 39 (4) (2008): 8, www.edf.org/documents/8225_Solutions_0808.pdf.

Cities doing their share: Seattle: King County Solid Waste Division, http://your.kingcounty.gov/solidwaste/garbage-recycling/recycle-food.asp.Lafayette: Sophie Braccini, "Food Scrap Recycling Giving Back to Nature," *Lamorindu Weekly*, July 25, 2007, 1. Lille: "From Plate to Engine: French City Powers Buses with Food Scraps," Agence France Presse, September 19, 2007.

Tom Furrer: Shelah Moody, "Petaluma Creek Burbles Again Thanks to High School Teacher and Students," *San Francisco Chronicle*, July 20, 2008.

Freecycle: See www.freecycle.org.

Friends of the Earth/Middle East: See www.foeme.org.

The New Green Mainstream: Hartman Group, "Food and the Environment: A Consumer's Perspective," 1997. See also Tibbett L. Speer, "Growing the Green Market," *American Demographics*, August, 1997. See also Paul H. Ray and Sherry Ruth Anderson, *The Cultural Creatives: How 50 Million People are Changing the World* (New York: Harmony Books, 2001).

Steward of the land: American Farmland Trust, "2008 Steward of the Land: Nash Huber of Nash's Organic Produce," www.farmland.org/programs/award/Winners-2008.asp.

Human demands have tripled since 1961: World Wildlife Fund, *Living Planet Report* (Gland, Switzerland: WWF International, 2006): 1.

Gap: Jeffrey M. Jones, "In the U.S., 28% Report Major Changes to Live Green," April 18, 2008, www.Gallup.com/poll/106624/US-28-Report-Major-Changes-Live-Green.aspx.

Technology—Boon or Bane?

Green revolution now brown: Daniel Pepper, "India's Green Revolution Gets Second Look," *San Francisco Chronicle*, July 28, 2008.

GPS: Sandra Postel, "Growing More Food with Less Water," *Scientific American*, February, 2001.

Fair tracing: See www.fairtracing.org.

Aid matrix: See www.aidmatrix.org.

In vitro meat: I. Datar and M. Betti, "Possibilities for an In Vitro Meat Production System," *Innovative Food Science and Emerging Technologies* 11(1) (2010): 13-22 [Abstract].

The scoop on poop: Elizabeth Rosenthal, "As More Eat Meat, a Bid to Cut Emissions," *New York Times,* December 4, 2008.

EPA program: See www.epa.gov/agstar/about-us/index.html.

Satellite surveillance: L. Coulibaly, "Africa Turns To Satellites To Curb Fish Poaching," Reuters, July 27, 2007.

"Bottling sunshine": Michelle Locke, "Vintners Bottle Sunshine with Solar Powered Harvest," Associated Press, September 27, 2007.

RecycleBank: Keith Naughton and Daniel McGinn, "Saving the World for a Latte," *Newsweek,* October 6, 2008.

Ancient methods revived: Christian Caryl, "Cool, Clear Water," *Newsweek,* October 1, 2007.

Solving a gas problem: Brita Belli, "Better Cow Burps," *E Magazine,* September 17, 2010, www.emagazine.com/view/?5333. See also Leslie Tamura, "Burping Cows Add to Climate Change," *Washington Post,* September 21, 2010, www.washingtonpost.com/wp-dyn/content/article/2010/09/20/AR2010092004819.html.

Marker-assisted selection: Union of Concerned Scientists, "High Yields From New Breeding Technique," *Food and Environment Electronic Digest,* January 8, 2008. See also Kansas State University press release, "Feeding the World without Genetic Engineering," September 28, 2007, and Richard Manning, "Super Organics," *Wired,* May, 2004.

Four Birds on One Branch
Yossi Leshem: Ben Winograd, "Barn Owls Unite Israelis, Jordanians," Associated Press, July 15, 2007. See also www.foeme.org.

Part I Your 5 Most Important Decisions
"Ecological restoration": Paul Hawken, *Blessed Unrest* (New York: Viking, 2007), 189.

Eat Food, Not Chemicals
The Truth about Pesticides
1 billion pounds a year: Earthjustice, "The Faces and Voices of Pesticide Poisoning," www.earthjustice.org/features/campaigns/the-faces-and-voices-of-pesticide-poisoning.

Crop losses: Pesticide Action Network, "Pesticides 101—A Primer," www.panna.org/issues/pesticides-101-primer.

"Pesticide treadmill": Lester R. Brown, Michael Renner, and Brian Halweil, *Vital Signs 1999* (New York: W. W. Norton, 1999), 124.

160 known or suspected carcinogens: Physicians for Social Responsibility, *Cancer and the Environment: What Health Care Providers Should Know* (Washington DC: PSR, 2002), 3. See also Physicians for Social Responsibility, *Environmental Endocrine Disruptors: What Health Care Providers Should Know* (Washington, DC: PSR, 2001).

Contamination of human milk: Francesco Massart et al., "Human Breast Milk and Xenoestrogen Exposure: A Possible Impact on Human Health," *Journal of Perinatology* 25 (4) (2005): 282-288 [Abstract].

Exporting banned pesticides: Carl Smith et al., "Pesticide Exports from U.S. Ports, 2001-2003," *International Journal of Occupational and Environmental Health* 14 (3) (2008): 176-186 [Abstract].

Only 1% inspected: Marian Burros, "Who's Watching What We Eat?" *New York Times,* May 16, 2007.

What the USDA labels mean: USDA, "Understanding Organic Labeling," February 5, 2010, www.ams.usda.gov at http://bit.ly/hNVeoQ.

Most important to buy organic: Elson Haas, *Staying Healthy Shopper's Guide: Feed Your Family Safely* (Berkeley, CA: Celestial Arts, 1999), 112-113. Also personal communication from Susan Kegley, Pesticide Action Network. See also Environmental Working Group, www.foodnews.org.

Definition of organic: USDA Sustainable Agriculture Research and Education (SARE), *Transitioning to Organic Production,* 2006, www.sare.org/publications/organic/or-ganic01.htm.

Organic and Health
Conventional produce less nutritious: Charles Benbrook et al., "New Evidence Confirms the Nutritional Superiority of Plant-Based Organic Foods," 2008, www.or-ganic-center.org/reportfiles/Nutrient_Content_SSR_Executive_Summary_FINAL.pdf. Also Alyson Mitchell et al., "Ten-Year Comparison of the Influence of Organic and Conventional Crop Management Practices on the Content of Flavonoids in Tomatoes," *Journal of Agricultural and Food Chemistry* 55 (15) (2007): 6154-6159 [Abstract]. See also Donald R. Davis, "Declining Fruit and Vegetable Nutrient Composition: What Is the Evidence?" *HortScience* 44 (2009): 15-19 [Abstract].

Real Organic vs. Greenwash
Some producers pretend to be green: Joel Makower, *State of Green Business 2008* (Oakland, CA: Greener World Media, 2008), 7. See also Charlotte Vallaeys et al., "Behind the Bean: The Heroes and Charlatans of the Natural and Organic Soy Foods Industry," *Cornucopia* Institute, 2009 [Executive Summary].

Greenpeace criteria: http://stopgreenwash.org/criteria.

Dairy processor stalled investigations: Mark Kastel, "Clout-Heavy Dean Foods Kills USDA Investigation of Their Horizon Label," *Cornucopia,* May 12, 2008.

Eat Lower on the Food Chain

The Protein Myth
Nutritionist Michele Vivas, personal communication, quoting Center for Science in the Public Interest.

The Truth about Meat
General description: Pew Commission on Industrial Farm Animal Production, "Putting Meat On The Table: Industrial Farm Animal Production in America" (2008) [Executive Summary], www.ncifap.org/bin/s/a/PCIFAPSmry.pdf.

Grain to produce meat: See Vaclav Smil, *Feeding the World: A Challenge for the Twenty-First Century* (Cambridge, MA: MIT Press, 2000), 157. See also Lester R. Brown, Michael Renner, and Brian Halweil, *Vital Signs 1999* (New York: W. W. Norton, 1999), 19. See also Robert Goodland and David Pimentel, "Environmental Sustainability and Integrity in the Agriculture Sector," in *Ecological Integrity: Integrating Environment, Conservation, and Health,* ed. David Pimentel, Laura Westra, and Reed. F. Noss (Washington, DC: Island Press, 2000).

What Are We Eating?
10 billion land animals: Humane Society of the United States, "Follow the Three Rs," 2006,www.humanesociety.org/assets/pdfs/farm/Three-Rs-05.pdf.

10 billion fish and 19,011 animals per minute: Melanie Joy, *Why We Love Dogs, Eat Pigs, and Wear Cows* (San Francisco, Conari Press, 2010), 37.

What about Hunger?
Fish catch goes to livestock: Jennifer Jacquet, "Farm Animals Consume 17% of Wild-Caught Fish," *Grist,* June 27, 2008, www.grist.org/article/fish-and-pigs-and-chickens-oh-my.

10 times as much grain: Rosamond Naylor of Stanford, quoted by Mark Bittman, "Rethinking the Meat-Guzzler," *New York Times,* January 27, 2008.

"If all the grain": Jim Motovalli, "The Meat of the Matter: Our Livestock Industry Creates More Greenhouse Gas Than Transportation Does," *E Magazine,* August 22, 2008.

Greenhouse Gases and Climate Change
Worldwide greenhouse gases: U.N. Food and Agriculture Organization, *Livestock's Long Shadow* (2006): 136. See also Humane Society of the United States, "The Impact of Animal Agriculture on Global Warming and Climate Change," 2008, www.humanesociety.org/assets/pdfs/farm/hsus-the-impact-of-animal-agriculture-on-global-warming-and-climate-change.pdf. See also Anthony J. McMichael et al., "Food, Livestock Production, Energy, Climate Change, and Health," *The Lancet* 370 (October 6, 2007): 1253-1263 [Abstract]. Also Dr. Julika Weiss of the Institute for Ecological Economy Research, personal communication.

"Living smokestacks": Elizabeth Rosenthal, "As More Eat Meat, a Bid to Cut Emissions," *New York Times,* December 14, 2008.

Don't Drive a Cow, Man
2 pounds of beef greenhouse gases: Daniele Fanelli, "Meat Is Murder on the Environment," *New Scientist,* 2007, www.newscientist.com/article/mg19526134.500-meat-is-murder-on-the-environment.html.

Camry vs. Prius: Gidon Eshel and Pamela A. Martin, "Diet Energy, and Global Warming," *Earth Interactions* 2006, Volume 10, Paper No. 9, http://pge.uchicago.edu/workshop/documents/martin1.pdf.

33 million automobiles: Center for Science in the Public Interest, quoted in Jim Motovalli, "The Meat of the Matter: Our Livestock Industry Creates More Greenhouse Gas Than Transportation Does," *E Magazine,* August 22, 2008.

Water
5 to 10 times: "E-Conference Synthesis: Virtual Water Trade—Conscious Choices" (World Water Council, 2004) 4.

50 times as much as eggs: Vaclav Smil, *Feeding the World: A Challenge for the Twenty-First Century* (Cambridge, MA: MIT Press, 2000), 160.

Water pollution: Nancy Lawson, "An Even More Inconvenient Truth," *All Animals* 10 (1) (2008): 10-13, citing U.N.'s FAO *Livestock's Long Shadow* report of 2006.

Manure
13 times the amount: EPA Office of Water, Standards, and Applied Science Division, "Environmental Impacts of Animal Feeding Operations," 1998, www.epa.gov/water-science/guide/feedlots/envimpct.pdf.

22 tons a year: Alexia Retallack, "California's Dairies: Where Product Quality and Environmental Integrity Meet," *Outdoor California* 60 (3) (1999): 20-24.

1,600 dairies: "Animal Waste Pollution in America, An Emerging National Problem:

Environmental Risks of Livestock and Poultry Production." Report compiled by the minority staff of the U.S. Senate Committee on Agriculture, Nutrition, and Forestry, December, 1997.

Oklahoma suing Arkansas chicken producers: Juliet Eilperin, "Pollution in the Water, Lawsuits in the Air," *Washington Post,* August 28, 2006.

Waco settlement from dairies: Christopher Law, "Oklahoma-Arkansas Dispute Exposes National Problem," *DC Bureau,* August 28, 2006.

A Cesspool by Any Other Name
Description: Nancy Lawson, "Transforming an Industry," *All Animals* 10 (20) (2008): 8-9.

Property values go down: Union of Concerned Scientists, "The Hidden Costs of CAFOs," *Earthwise* (Spring, 2009): 2. See also Doug Gurian-Sherman, "CAFOs Uncovered: The Untold Costs of Confined Animal Feeding Operations," Union of Concerned Scientists report, 2008.

Or maybe you *should* drive a cow ... .. Edward Humes, "The Latest from the Labs," *Sierra,* September-October, 2010. See also www.harvestcleanenergy.org/conference/HCE7/PDFs/Leonhardt.pdf.

Antibiotics
Resistance: Alicia D. Anderson et al., "Public Health Consequences of Use of Antimicrobial Agents in Food Animals in the United States" *Microbial Drug Resistance* 9 (4) (2003): 373-379 [Abstract].

70% of antibiotics resistant: Mary C. Pearl, "Antibiotic Use on the Farm Hurts Human Health–And it Doesn't Even Help the Bottom Line," *Discover,* September, 2007.

"Meat equivalent of Miracle Gro": Paul Roberts, "The Cost of Steak," *Los Angeles Times,* August 23, 2008.

Over two thirds of antibiotics given to livestock: Union of Concerned Scientists, "70% of All Antibiotics Given to Healthy Livestock," January 8, 2001. See www.ucsusa.org.

Agencies clamping down: Katherine Shea, Karen Florini, and Tamar Barlam, *When Wonder Drugs Don't Work: How Antibiotic Resistance Threatens Children, Seniors, and the Medically Vulnerable* (Washington, DC: Environmental Defense, 2001).

$1.5 to $3 billion a year public health costs: Union of Concerned Scientists, "The Hidden Costs of CAFOs," *Earthwise* (Spring, 2009): 2. See also Doug Gurian-Sherman, "CAFOs Uncovered: The Untold Costs Of Confined Animal Feeding Operations," Union of Concerned Scientists report, 2008.

"The trouble with factory farms": Editorial, "Antibiotic Runoff," *New York Times,* September 18, 2007.

Hormones
Age of puberty: Sandra Steingraber, *The Falling Age of Puberty in U.S. Girls: What We Know, What We Need to Know* (San Francisco: Breast Cancer Fund, 2007).

Land and Biodiversity
Description: Barbara McDonald, "Crossing the Species Boundary and Natural Resource Management" (paper presented at the 8th International Symposium on Society and Resource Management. Bellingham, WA. June 17-22, 2000). See also Center for Biological Diversity, "Grazing," www.biologicaldiversity.org/programs/public_lands/grazing/index.html.

Keystone critters: Defenders of Wildlife, "Prairie Dogs Moved to Safer Ground at Thunder Basin," www.defenders.org/about_us/success_stories /prairie_dogs_moved_to_safer_ground_at_thunder_basin.php.

Well-managed ranches: Union of Concerned Scientists, "What Is a Smart Pasture Operation?" August 23, 2008, www.ucsusa.org/food_and_agriculture/solutions / smart_pasture_operations/ what-is-a-smart-pasture.html.

Your Tax Dollar

Cleaning up environmental damage: Doug Gurian-Sherman, "CAFOs Uncovered: The Untold Costs of Confined Animal Feeding Operations," Union Of Concerned Scientists Report, 2008.

$245 billion dollars in farm subsidies: Environmental Working Group, Farm Subsidy Database, "The United States Summary Information," http://farm.ewg.org/region.php?fips=00000.

$1.35 a month per cow and calf: Center for Biological Diversity, "Grazing," www.biologicaldiversity.org/programs/public_lands/grazing/index.html.

Subsidies: Physicians Committee for Responsible Medicine, "Health vs. Pork: Congress Debates the Farm Bill," *Good Medicine,* Autumn 2007, www.pcrm.org/magazine/gm07autumn/health_pork.html.

Not too many, not too few: American Farmland Trust, "AFT Awardee Embraces Stewardship," www.farmland.org/programs/campaign/voices/Sinton.asp.

Meat and Human Health

Heart disease: A.M. Bernstein et al., "Major Dietary Protein Sources and Risk of Coronary Heart Disease in Women," *Circulation* 111 (9) (2010): 876-883 [Abstract]. See also R. Micha et al., "Red and Processed Meat Consumption and Risk of Incident Coronary Heart Disease, Stroke, and Diabetes Mellitus: A Systematic Review and Meat-Analysis," *Circulation* 121 (21) (2010): 2271-2283 [Abstract].

Infertility: J.E. Chavarro et al., "Protein Intake and Ovulatory Infertility," *American Journal of Obstetric Gynecology* 198 (2008): 210e1–210e7 [Abstract].

Breast cancer: Janet Gray, "State of the Evidence: The Connection Between Breast Cancer and the Environment," Breast Cancer Fund 6th edition, 2010. See also Eunyoung Cho, "Premenopausal Fat Intake and Risk of Breast Cancer," *Journal of the National Cancer Institute* 95 (2003): 1079–85.

Lung, esophagus, and liver: A.J. Cross et al., "A Prospective Study of Red and Processed Meat Intake in Relation to Cancer Risk," *PLoS Medicine* 4(12) (2007): e325.

Colon/rectum: S.C Larsson and A. Wolk, "Meat Consumption and Risk of Colorectal Cancer: A Meta-Analysis of Prospective Studies," *International Journal of Cancer* 119 (110) (2006): 2657-2664 [Abstract]. See also A. Flood et al., "Dietary Patterns as Identified by Factor Analysis and Colorectal Cancer Among Middle-Aged Americans," *American Journal of Clinical Nutrition* 88 (1) (2008): 176-184 [Abstract].

Vegetarian diet and less obesity: P.R. Newby et al., "Risk of Overweight and Obesity Among Semivegetarian, Lactovegetarian, and Vegan Women," *Journal of Clinical Nutrition* 81 (2005): 1267-74 [Abstract].

"The results of an evidence-based review": "Position of the American Dietetic Association: Vegetarian Diets," *Journal of the American Dietetic Association* 109 (7) (2009): 1266-1282. See www.eatright.org/about/content.aspx?id=8357.

"The lacto-ovo vegetarian diet": David Pimentel and Marcia Pimentel, "Sustainability of Meat-Based and Plant-Based Diets and the Environment," *American Journal of Clinical Nutrition* 78 (supplement) (2003): 660S-663S.

Prescription Produce: Natasha Singer, "Eat an Apple (Doctor's Orders)," *New York Times*, August 12, 2010.

Dairy and Eggs
Parkinson's: H. Chen et al., "Consumption of Dairy Products and Risk of Parkinson's Disease," *American Journal of Epidemiology* 165 (9) (2007): 998-1006 [Abstract].

Breast cancer: E. Cho et al., "Premenopausal Fat Intake and Risk of Breast Cancer," *Journal of the National Cancer Institute* 95 (14) (2003): 1079-1085 [Abstract].

Ovarian cancer: S.C. Larsson et al., "Milk, Milk Products, and Lactose Intake and Ovarian Cancer Risk: A Meta-Analysis of Epidemiological Studies," *International Journal of Cancer* 118 (2) (2006): 431-441 [Abstract].

Insulin resistance and metabolic syndrome: D.A Lawlor et al., "Avoiding Milk Is Associated with a Reduced Risk of Insulin Resistance and the Metabolic Syndrome," *Diabetic Medicine* 22 (6) (2005): 808-811 [Abstract]. See also M Goldfarb, "Relation of Time of Introduction of Cow Milk Protein to an Infant And Risk of Type 1 Diabetes Mellitus," *Journal of Proteome Research* 7 (2008): 2165-2167.

Fish
By the middle of this century: Boris Worm et al., "Impacts of Biodiversity Loss on Ocean Ecosystem Services," *Science* 314 (November 3, 2006): 787-790. See also Jacqueline Alder et al., "Forage Fish: From Ecosystems to Markets," *Annual Review of Environment and Resources* 33 (2008): 7.1-7.14.

Overfishing
Overfishing: Michael Berrill, *The Plundered Seas: Can the World's Fish be Saved?* (San Francisco: Sierra Club, 1997). See also Jeremy B. C. Jackson et al., "Historical Overfishing and the Recent Collapse of Coastal Ecosystems" *Science* 293 (July 27, 2001): 629-638, and Casson Trenor, *Carting Away the Oceans: How Grocery Stores Are Emptying Our Seas* (Washington DC: Greenpeace, 2010).

"Underwater clear-cutting": John S. Rosenberg, "Of Ants and Earth," *Harvard Magazine*, March-April, 2003, 36-41.

Fish getting smaller: Laura Helmuth, "Our Imperiled Oceans: Seeing Is Believing," *Smithsonian*, September, 2008. See also Jeffrey A. Hutchings, "Collapse and Recovery of Marine Fishes," *Nature* 406 (2000): 882-885. See also Daniel Pauly et al., "Fishing Down Aquatic Food Webs," *American Scientist* 88 (1) (2000): 46-51. See also Greenbiz, "Supermarkets Failing to Adopt Sustainable Seafood Buying Practices," June 18, 2008, www.greenbiz.com/news/2008/06/17/supermarkets-failing-adopt-sustainable-seafood-buying-practices-report.

Dredges: Consumers Union, "America's Fish: Fair or Foul?" *Consumer Reports*, February, 2001.

Mudtrails: "Bottom Trawling Impacts on Ocean, Clearly Visible from Space," *Science Daily*, February 20, 2008, www.sciencedaily.com/releases/2008/02/080215121207.htm.

85% of species in Mediterranean: Nicole Itano, "On Emptying Seas, A Vanishing Way of Life," *Christian Science Monitor*, January 16, 2008.

European fleets sent to Africa: Sharon Lafraniere, "Europe Takes Africa's Fish, and Boatloads of Migrants Follow," *New York Times*, January 14, 2008.

Cod fishery has yet to recover: World Resources Institute, *Millennium Ecosystem Assessment: Living Beyond Our Means* (Washington, DC: World Resources Institute, 2005), 18.

72,000 jobs lost: Environmental Defense, "Sustaining America's Fisheries and Fishing Communities," 2007, www.edf.org/documents/6119_sustainingfisheries.pdf, Executive Summary, 2.

Catch share programs: www.sustainingfisheries.com; Environmental Defense, "For Fishing Communities, a Bridge over Troubled Waters," *Solutions* 38 (3) (2007): 4; also "A Lifeline for Gulf Fishermen," *Solutions* 41(3) (2010): 10, www.edf.org/documents/11322_Solutions-fall-2010.pdf. See also Environmental Defense Special Report, "Turning the Tide: Fishermen Embrace a New Approach to End Overfishing" (Fall, 2010). See also Christopher Costello et al., "Can Catch Shares Prevent Fisheries Collapse?" *Science* 321 (September 19, 2008): 1678-1681 [Abstract].

Sea Change Investment Fund: Ilana deBare, "Cleanfish: Helping the Small Fish Make It in Big Marketing Pond," *San Francisco Chronicle*, August 10, 2008. See also Ilana deBare, "Sea Change: Venture Fund Is Sold on Focusing on Sustainability," *San Francisco Chronicle*, August 10, 2008.

Clean Fish: See www.cleanfish.com. See also "America's Most Promising Social Entrepreneurs," *Bloomberg Businessweek*, April 3, 2009, http://images.businessweek.com/ss/09/04/0403_social_entrepreneurs/5.htm.

Bycatch and Competition

Dolphins in Japan: Personal communication, Andy Snow. See also Environmental Investigating Agency, "Japan's Seas Run Red in Annual Porpoise Hunt," March 10, 2010, www.eia-international.org/cgi/news/news.cgi?t=template&a=583.

For every pound of shrimp: "Biodiversity and Your Food: Did You Know?" American Museum of Natural History, http://cbc.amnh.org/living/food/index.html.

Big Business and the Golden Goose

"You are thinking": Donella H. Meadows, Dennis L. Meadows, and Jorgen Randers, *Beyond the Limits: Confronting Global Collapse, Envisioning a Sustainable Future* (White River Junction, VT: Chelsea Green, 1992), 187-188.

"Fishing in the ocean is no longer sustainable": "When Will We Tame the Oceans?" *Nature,* 436 (July 14, 2005): 175-176.

Dead Zones and Dams

Runoff flows to oceans: Sarah Simpson, "Shrinking the Dead Zone," *Scientific American,* July, 2001.

Dead zones around the world: R. J. Diaz and R. Rosenberg, "Spreading Dead Zones and Consequences for Marine Ecosystems," *Science* 321 (August 15, 2008): 926-929.

Gulf of Mexico Dead Zone 7,900 square miles: Dan Ferber, "Keeping the Stygian Waters at Bay," *Science* 291 (February 9, 2001): 968-973.

Dams and salmon: Fen Montaigne, "A River Dammed," *National Geographic* 199 (4) (April, 2001): 2-33.

Manatawny Creek: EPA, "Pennsylvania: Manatawny Creek and Tributary Stream Restoration, Dam Removal Restore Waterbodies," www.epa.gov/owow/NPS/success/state/pa_man.htm.

Buying the Dams: Penobscot River: Penobscot River Restoration Trust, "Penobscot River Restoration Trust Purchases Three Dams from PPL Corp." www.penobscotriver.

org. See also Madeline Bodin, "Freeing the River," *Nature Conservancy* 60 (2) (2010): 32-41.

Poisoned Streams and Oceans Threaten our Health

Mercury and birth defects: Bob Ludwig, "EPA's Methylmercury Guideline Is Scientifically Justifiable for Protecting Most Americans But Some May Be at Risk," Press release from the National Academy of Sciences, July 11, 2000. See also "Methylmercury's Toxic Toll," *Science News* 158 (2000): 77.

Gold miners: Jim Doyle, "Hydraulic Gold Mining Blamed for Mercury-Poisoned Fish," *San Francisco Chronicle*, September 27, 2000. See also John Krist, "Gold Rush Leaves State Toxic Legacy," *Ventura County Star,* May 12, 2001.

New York restaurants test for mercury: Marian Burros, "More Testing of Seafood to Address Mercury Concerns," *New York Times,* January 30, 2008.

Compassion in action: John Heilprin, "Shark Attack Survivors Don't Forget but Do Forgive," Associated Press, September 13, 2010.

Fish Farming

Two or three pounds of wild fish: Ed Stoddard, "Eating Fish: Good for Heart, Bad for Environment?" Reuters, August 10, 2007. See also S. Milius, "Carnivorous Fish Nibble at Farming Again," *Science News* 158 (July 1, 2000), 7.

Five to one: R.L. Naylor et al., "Effect of Aquaculture on World Fish Supplies," *Nature* 405 (2000): 1017-1024. See also Julio E. Perez et al., "Aquaculture: Part of the Problem, Not a Solution," *Nature* 408 (November 30, 2000): 514.

Net protein loss: Editorial, "The Protein Pyramid," *New York Times,* November 10, 2008.

Coastal forests and wetlands destroyed: Vaclav Smil, *Feeding the World: A Challenge for the Twenty-First Century* (Cambridge: MIT, 2000), 177. See also Isabel de la Torre, "The Unpalatable Prawn," *Earth Island Journal* (Spring, 2000): 28.

Tuna ranches. Richard Ellis, "The Bluefin in Peril," *Scientific American,* March, 2008.

Treaties poorly enforced: Daniel Jack Chasen, "The Rusted Shield: Government's Failure to Enforce–Or Obey–Our System of Environmental Laws," Report commissioned by the Bullitt Foundation, 2000. See also "Experts Call For Halt to Bluefin Tuna Fishing in Mediterranean," Agence France Presse, September 11, 2008.

Japan's whale "research": C. Scott Baker et al., "Scientific Whaling: Source of Illegal Products for Market?" *Science* 290 (December 1, 2000): 1695-1696. See also Dennis Normile, "Japan's Whaling Program Carries Heavy Baggage," *Science* 289 (September 29, 2000): 2264-2265.

Sanctuaries not guarded: Janet Raloff, "Underwater Refuge," *Science News* 159 (April 28, 2001): 264-266.

Pirates ignore treaties: Lester R. Brown, Michael Renner, and Brian Halweil, *Vital Signs 1999* (New York: W. W. Norton, 1999), 36.

20 nations agreed to restrict: "Nations to Limit South Pacific Trawling," *The Washington Post,* May 5, 2007.

Walmart sustainable shrimp: http://walmartstores.com/media/factsheets/fs_2248.pdf.

3.8 million acres: Colin Woodard, "Saving Fish and a Fishing Industry: 3.8 Million Acres off California Protected from Trawling," *The Nature Conservancy Magazine,* 2008, www.nature.org/magazine/autumn2006/misc/art18615.html.

Sustainable tuna fishery: "World's First Sustainable Tuna Fishery Certified," *Focus*, January-February, 2008, 1.

California Fishers Fund: "A Lifeline for California Fishermen," Environmental Defense Annual Report (2007), 21.

Avoid Chilean sea bass: Monterey Bay Aquarium, www.montereybayaquarium.org/cr/seafoodwatch.aspx.

Who ya gonna call? :Katherine Harmon, "Sustainable Fishing at Your Fingertips," *Scientific American*, January, 2009. See also www.blueocean.org/files/FishPhone_ContestDetails.pdf.

More Humanely Raised Meat, Dairy, and Eggs
Conditions in factory farms: Doug Gurian-Sherman, "CAFOs Uncovered: The Untold Costs of Confined Animal Feeding Operations," Union of Concerned Scientists report, 2008. See also Melanie Joy *Why We Love Dogs, Eat Pigs, and Wear Cows* (San Francisco: Conari Press, 2010).

Compass Group: Nancy Lawson, "Transforming an Industry," *All Animals* 10 (20) (2008): 8-9.

"Every hour in the U.S.": The Humane Society of the United States, "Humane Eating and the Three Rs." See www.hsus.org/farm/humaneeating.

Eat Shorter on the Food Chain
1,500 miles: R. Pirog, T. Van Pelt, K. Enshayan, and E. Cook, *Food, Fuel, and Freeways: An Iowa Perspective on How Far Food Travels, Fuel Usage, and Greenhouse Gas Emissions* (Ames, IA: Leopold Center for Sustainable Agriculture, 2001).

The Global Cornucopia and its Cost to the Earth
Bees from Australia: Singeli Agnew, "The Almond and the Bee," *San Francisco Chronicle*, October 14, 2007.

Fish from Norway: Elisabeth Rosenthal, "Movable Feast Carries a Pollution Price Tag," *New York Times*, April 26, 2008; See also Sarah Murray, "Sacred and Mundane from Ocean to Plate, A Posthumous Migration," *Orion*, 2007, www.orionmagazine.org/index.php/mag/issue/452.

"Global supply chains have grown so long": Nicholas Zamiska and David Kesmodel, "Tainted Ginger's Long Trip from China to U.S. Stores," *Wall Street Journal*, November 19, 2007.

1,000 fewer miles a year: Ewen Callaway, "Food Miles Don't Feed Climate Change–Meat Does," www.NewScientist.com, April 18, 2008.

The Adventure of the Curious Locavore
"Distance is the enemy": A. Smith and J.B. MacKinnon, *Plenty: One Man, One Woman, and a Raucous Year of Eating Locally* (New York: Harmony Books, 2007).

$7 billion by 2011: "Locally Grown Foods Niche Cooks Up at $5 Billion as America Chows Down on Fresh," *Packaged Facts*, June 20, 2007.

University of Vermont: University Dining Services, "Sustainability," http://uds.uvm.edu/social.html.

Big and local: See www.bamco.com.

Critics: James E. McWilliams, "Food That Travels Well," *New York Times*, August 6, 2007.

Life cycle: Sarah Murray, "The Deep-Fried Truth," *New York Times,* December 14, 2007. See also Sarah deWeerdt, "Is Local Food Better?" www.worldwatch.org/node/6064.

Stretching the definition: Kim Severson, "When 'Local' Makes it Big," *New York Times,* May 13, 2009.

Eliminating meat is even more powerful: Christopher Weber and Scott Matthews, "Food-Miles and the Relative Climate Impacts of Food Choices in the U.S." *Environmental Science and Technology* 42 (10) (2008): 3508-3513 [Abstract].

What's green and grows in all 50 states?: Sharon Rolenc, "Minnesota Schools 'Digging' their Local Farmers This Week," Public News Service, 2010. See also www.publicnews-service.org/index.php?/content/article/16096-1 and www.farmtoschool.org.

Fresh food in season: Jessica Prentice, *Full Moon Feast: Food and the Hunger for Connection* (White River Junction, VT: Chelsea Green, 2006).

Support Your Local Farmer

2,500 CSAs: See www.localharvest.org/csa/

Pike Place. Ron Strochlic and Crispin Shelley, "Community Supported Agriculture in California, Oregon, and Washington: Challenges and Opportunities," 2004, Report from California Institute for Rural Studies, funded by USDA, www.cirsinc.org/Sustain-ableFoodSystems.html.

Persuasive locavore: "New American Dream and Designer Jim Pollack Make One Family's Dreams Come True," Press release from New American Dream, September 12, 2007, http://bit.ly/hOB6xz.

Eat Wider on the Food Chain

Diversity in Danger

¾ of world's calories: Paul Hawken, Amory Lovins, and L. Hunter Lovins, *Natural Capitalism: Creating the Next Industrial Revolution* (Boston: Little, Brown, 1999), 194.

Corn fungus, 1970: American Museum of Natural History, "What's the Connection between What We Buy and Biodiversity?" http://cbc.amnh.org/living/buy/connection.html.

"Seeds are the software": John Archer, "Arctic Vault Takes Shape for World Food Crops," Reuters, September 20, 2007.

Eccentrics to the Rescue

Tuscan crops abandoned: Elizabeth Rosenthal, "Plant Diversity Future May Depend on Europe's Backyard Gardeners," *San Francisco Chronicle,* December 1, 2007.

Wine detective: Aaron Maines, "Italy's Ancient Vines," *Wall Street Journal,* July 5-6, 2008.

Potato rainbow: International Potato Center (Centro Internacional de la Papa), www.cipotato.org.

Diversity in Protein

20% of livestock endangered: U.N. Food and Agriculture Organization, "Special: Biodiversity for Food and Agriculture–Farm Animal Genetic Resources," February, 1998, www.fao.org/sd/epdirect/epre0042.htm.

Eating insects: William F. Lyon, "Insects as Human Food," Ohio State University Extension Fact Sheet HYG 2160-96. See also Peter Menzel and Faith D'Aluisio, *Man Eating Bugs: The Art and Science of Eating Insects* (Berkeley, CA: Ten Speed Press,

1998) and David George Gordon, *The Eat-a-Bug Cookbook* (Berkeley, CA: Ten Speed Press, 1998).

Diversity in Sweeteners
16% of our calories: USDA, "What We Eat in America," www.ars.usda.gov/Services/docs.htm?docid=13793. Also see Center for Science in the Public Interest, "America: Drowning in Sugar," August 3, 1999, www.cspinet.org/new/sugar.html. See also Pat Kendall, "Sweet Talk: Moderating Your Sugar Intake," Colorado State University Cooperative Extension, May 22, 2001.

The Fat of the Land?
Obesity statistic: Centers for Disease Control and Prevention, "Vital Signs: State-Specific Obesity Prevalence Among Adults—United States, 2009," *Morbidity and Mortality Weekly Report*, August 3, 2010, www.cdc.gov/mmwr/preview/mmwrhtml/mm59e0803a1.htm?s_cid=mm59e0803a1_w.

Obesity, many causes: Kim Hiatt, Linda Riebel, and Harris Friedman, "The Gap Between What We Know and What We Do About Childhood Obesity: A Multi-Factor Model for Assessment, Intervention, and Prevention," *Journal of Social, Behavioral, and Health Sciences 1* (1) (2007): 1-44. Online at www.jsbhs.org/9049_24322.htm.

Noah's archives: Global Crop Diversity Trust, "Svalbard Global Seed Vault," www.croptrust.org/main/arcticseedvault.php?itemid=211.

Nude Food

Less Packaging
Andy Keller: Ilana DeBare, "Bag Business: Green Entrepreneurs Retool Humble Grocery Sack," *San Francisco Chronicle*, December 21, 2007.

Environnement Jeunesse: See www.enjeu.qc.ca.

215 billion beverage containers a year: Jon Mooallem, "The Unintended Consequences of Hyperhydration," *New York Times*, May 25, 2007.

Great Pacific Garbage Patch: National Oceanic and Atmospheric Administration, "Demystifying the 'Great Pacific Garbage Patch,'" http://marinedebris.noaa.gov/info/patch.html#5.

BPA: Tara Parker-Pope, "A Hard Plastic Is Raising Hard Questions," *New York Times*, April 22, 2008.

Health problems of BPA: Evanthia Diamanti-Kandarakis et al., "Endocrine-Disrupting Chemicals: An Endocrine Society Scientific Statement," *Endocrine Reviews* 30 (4) (2009): 293-342.

A little quiz: Tyler Colman (2008), "Drink Outside the Box," *New York Times*, August 18, 2008.

Less Processing
French fries: In this section, I am indebted to the books by John C. Ryan and Alan Thein Durning, *Stuff: The Secret Life of Everyday Things* (Seattle: Northwest Environment Watch, 1997) and Eric Schlosser, *Fast Food Nation: The Dark Side of the All-American Meal* (New York: Houghton Mifflin, 2001).

"Choreography of ingredients": Michael Pollan, "Behind the Organic-Industrial Complex," *New York Times*, May 13, 2001.

Eat less junk food: "Eating Less Meat and Junk Food Could Cut Fossil Energy Fuel

Use Almost in Half," *Science Daily,* July 24, 2008, www.sciencedaily.com/releases/2008/07/080723094838.htm.

Less Waste

$48 billion is wasted by households: World Business Council for Sustainable Development, "Wasted Food Is Also Wasted Water," Environmental News Network, www.enn.com/top_stories/article/38000.

1 hamburger takes 600 gallons of water: World Wildlife Fund, "How Much Water Does It Take To Produce Common Products?" *Focus* (May/June, 2009): 5.

New Jersey food waste digester: Evelyn Lee, "Profits from Wasted Food," *New Jersey Biz,* April 21, 2008.

Waste? Not a concept: Personal communication.

Glamour Water and its Sins

Multi-billion-dollar-a-year industry: National Resources Defense Council, "Bottled Water: Pure Drink or Pure Hype?" www.nrdc.org/water/drinking/bw/exesum.asp.

8.8 billion gallons in 2007: National Resources Defense Council, quoted in Rob Lever, "Bottled Water Debate Hits a Boiling Point, Agence France Presse, June 29, 2008; also Environmental Working Group, "Harmful Chemicals Found in Bottled Water," October 15, 2008.

25,000 bottles a year: Tali Arbel, "Feeling Thrifty, the Thirsty Reach for Tap Water," *San Francisco Chronicle,* June 18, 2008.

5 billion bottles a year, recycle only 25%: Marc Gunther, "The End of Garbage," *Fortune,* March, 2007. See also Jon Mooallem, "The Unintended Consequences of Hyperhydration," *New York Times,* May 25, 2007.

86% become litter or garbage: Emily Arnold, "Bottled Water: Pouring Resources Down the Drain," Earth Policy Institute, February 2, 2006, quoting Container Recycling Institute.

1.5 million barrels of oil: Alex Williams, "Water, Water Everywhere, But Guilt by the Bottleful," *New York Times,* August 12, 2007.

2.5 million tons of carbon dioxide, Pacific Institute quoted by Mark Boslet, "Bottled Water's Impact on Environment," *San Jose Mercury News,* December 16, 2007.

Thousands of miles. Elizabeth Royte, *Bottlemania: How Water Went on Sale and Why We Bought It* (New York: Bloomsbury, 2008).

Less pure than tap: Environmental Working Group, "Harmful Chemicals Found in Bottled Water," October 15, 2008, www.ewg.org/BottledWater/Bottled-Water-Quality-Investigation/NewsRelease.

"The rationale": Marian Burros, "Fighting the Tide, a Few Restaurants Tilt to Tap Water," *New York Times,* May 30, 2007.

San Francisco banned bottled water: Mark Boslet, "Bottled Water's Impact on Environment," *San Jose Mercury News,* December 16, 2007. See also Christopher Heredia, "Water Fight," *San Francisco Chronicle,* October 11, 2007.

Groundwater a commonly owned resource: Felicity Barringer, "Bottling Plan Pushes Groundwater to Center Stage in Vermont," *New York Times,* August 21, 2008.

Part II Finding Earth-Friendly Food

"Green is the new red, white, and blue": Thomas L. Friedman, "The Power of Green," *New York Times,* August 15, 2007.

Grocery Stores

Whole Foods scores high on sustainable fish: Casson Trenor, *Carting Away the Oceans: How Grocery Stores Are Emptying Our Seas* (Washington DC: Greenpeace, 2010).

Green Power Partner: Environment News Service, "EPA Salutes 18 Green Power Partners: Banks, Cities, Corporations and a Zoo," 2010, www.ens-newswire.com/ens/oct2010/2010-10-21-092.html.

The really green grocer: Erin Killian, "It's Not Easy Being Green," *Washington Business Journal,* July 21, 2006.

Farmers' Markets and Roadside Stands

Over 6,000 farmers markets: USDA, Agricultural Marketing Service, "Farmers Markets and Local Food Marketing," www.ams.usda.gov/AMSv1.0/FARMERSMARKETS.

Restaurants

Fast food. $100 billion: Eric Schlosser, *Fast Food Nation: The Dark Side of the All-American Meal* (New York: Houghton Mifflin, 2001), 3.

Best of all: Chefs Collaborative. See www.chefscollaborative.org.

Brooklyn bicycle: Deirdre Donovan, "Five Paths to a Greener Restaurant," *Zagat Buzz,* August 24, 2007.

Early adopter: See www.noras.com.

Caterers

Earth-friendly ever after: Jennifer Hattam, *Sierra* (May-June, 2007): 31; Mireya Navarro, "How Green Was My Wedding," *New York Times,* February 11, 2007; Kristin Dizon, "Nice Day for a Green Wedding," *Seattle Post-Intelligencer,* July 21, 2007.

Picnicking, Camping, and the Back Yard Barbecue

2,300 acres of forest: Oak Ridge National Laboratory, "Fourth of July No Picnic for the Nation's Environment," www.ornl.gov/info/press_releases/get_press_release.cfm?ReleaseNumber=mr20030703-00.

Gourmet dirt: SFEnvironment.org, "Our City's Programs, Composting," www.sfenvironment.org/our_programs/topics.html?ti=6. Also Robert Haley, personal communication.

At Work, at Play, and on the Road

Zoos: American Zoo and Aquarium Association at www.aza.org.

Take me out to the food fair: See www.cuesa.org.

Bioneers conference: "Connecting for Change: Guardians for Future Generations," Bioneers 2006 Yearbook, 22.

Coffee, Wine, and Other Beverages

Tyler Colman: Andrea Thompson, "The Carbon Footprint of Wine," *Live Science,* November 10, 2008.

60% of aluminum: Paul Hawken, Amory Lovins, and L. Hunter Lovins, *Natural Capitalism: Creating the Next Industrial Revolution* (Boston: Little, Brown, 1999), 50.

Coffee growing and processing: This paragraph draws heavily on John C. Ryan and Alan Thein Durning, *Stuff: The Secret Life of Everyday Things* (Seattle: Northwest Environment Watch, 1997).

Birds: National Resources Defense Council, "Coffee, Conservation, and Commerce in the Western Hemisphere," www.nrdc.org/health/farming/ccc/chap4.asp.

Part III Meals at Home
"The kitchen is the center": Annie Berthold Bond, *The Green Kitchen Handbook* (New York: HarperCollins, 1997), 1.

Use Energy Skillfully
Refrigerator biggest energy user: Michael Brower and Warren Leon, *Consumer's Guide to Effective Environmental Choices* (New York: Three Rivers Press, 1999), 68-69.

2009 Energy Star savings: EPA, "Energy Star Overview of 2009 Achievements," https://www.energystar.gov/ia/partners/annualreports/2009_achievements.pdf.

Use Water Wisely
Agriculture uses 2/3 of water: World Wildlife Fund, *Focus,* 31 (3) (May-June, 2009): 4. See also Nels Johnson et al., "Managing Water for People and Nature," *Science* 292 (May 11, 2001): 1071-1072.

Almost as much as we use: Donella H. Meadows, Dennis L. Meadows, and Jorgen Randers. *Beyond the Limits: Confronting Global Collapse, Envisioning a Sustainable Future* (White River Junction, VT: Chelsea Green, 1992), 56.

14% lost in leaks: See www.awwa.org/Resources/content.cfm?ItemNumber=29269&navItemNumber=1561.

Ogallala aquifer: Jane Braxton Little, "The Ogallala Aquifer: Saving a Vital U.S. Water Source," *Scientific American,* March, 2009.

Water to produce meat: Thomas Kostigen, "Virtual Water," *Discover,* June, 2008.

South of the border. See www.goldmanprize.org/2008/northamerica.

Reduce Waste
Over 90 billion pounds: Linda Scott Kantor et al., "Estimating and Addressing America's Food Losses," www.ers.usda.gov/Publications/FoodReview/Jan1997/Jan97a.pdf.

World War II: California Environmental Protection Agency Integrated Waste Management Board, *The Illustrated History of Recycling,* 1997, www.p2pays.org/ref/26/25070.pdf.

One cup of coffee: Thomas Kostigen, "Virtual Water," *Discover,* June, 2008.

One egg, World Wildlife Fund, "How Much Water Does It Take to Produce Common Products?" *Focus,* May-June 2009, 31 (3), 5. See also World Business Council for Sustainable Development, "Wasted Food is also Wasted Water," Environmental News Network, August 22, 2008.

Share the Bounty
1 billion hungry people: David Pimentel and Marcia Pimentel, "To Improve Nutrition for the World's Population," *Science* 288, (June 16, 2000): 1966-1967.

Clean Up Harmlessly

100% recycled paper towels: www.seventhgeneration.com.

#1 Best Company on the Planet: Ellis Jones, *The Better World Shopping Guide* (Gabriola Island, BC: New Society, 2006).

Annie Berthold Bond, *Clean and Green: The Complete Guide to Non-Toxic and Environmentally Safe Housekeeping* (Woodstock, NY: Ceres Press, 1994).

Maximize Materials by Recycling

245 million tons: EPA, "Recycling and Reuse–Reducing Our Waste and Resource Use," www.epa.gov/region1/green/recyclingandreuse.html.

58 Boeing 747s: National Resources Defense Council, "Trash Landings: How Airlines and Airports Can Clean Up their Recycling Programs," 2006, www.nrdc.org/trashlandings.

Recycling 82 million tons: EPA, "Municipal Solid Waste Generation, Recycling, and Disposal in the United States: Facts and Figures for 2006," www.epa.gov/epaoswer/non-hw/muncpl/facts.htm.

Recycling employs 1.1 million people: Marc Gunther, "The End of Garbage," *Fortune*, March, 2007.

Prevent hardening of the pipelines: Charles Burress, "Greasy Path to a Clean Future," *San Francisco Chronicle*, November 20, 2007. See also Carolyn Jones, "From Grease to Fuel," *San Francisco Chronicle*, December 28, 2008, and www.sfgreasecycle.org.

Build Topsoil by Composting

Confessions of a wormophile: Lawrence Downes, "A Box of Worms," *New York Times*, September 7, 2007.

"Do the rot thing": See www.stopwaste.org.

Part IV Join the Movement

"Suddenly, everywhere I look": Deborah Rich, "Cooking Up a Delectable Feast for the Body and the Soul," *San Francisco Chronicle*, August 23, 2008.

Sustainable and More Humane Agriculture

Koan: James Prichard, "Hogs Help Battle Beetle In Apple Orchard," Associated Press, March 5, 2008; also personal communication from Jim Koan.

"Unlike industrial agriculture": Michael Brower and Warren Leon, *Consumer's Guide to Effective Environmental Choice* (New York: Three Rivers Press, 1997), 97.

No-till: David Huggins and John Reganold, "No-till: The Quiet Revolution," *Scientific American*, July, 2008. Also David Montgomery, "Pay Dirt," *Scientific American*, July, 2008.

Integrated pest management. EPA, "Integrated Pest Management (IPM) Principles," www.epa.gov/pesticides/factsheets/ipm.htm.

Ceago Vinegarden: Lisa McLaughlin, "Virtuous Vino," *Time*, February 22, 2007.

Biointensive: John Jeavons, *How to Grow More Vegetables*, 6th Revised Edition (Berkeley, Ten Speed Press, 2002).

One farm could feed 200-300 families: Gidon Eshel and Pamela Martin, quoted in article from *Science Daily*, "Study: Vegan Diets Healthier for Planet, People Than Meat Diets," April 14, 2006, www.sciencedaily.com/releases/2006/04/060414012755.htm.

CAFOs: Doug Gurian-Sherman, "CAFOs Uncovered: The Untold Costs of Confined Animal Feeding Operations," Union of Concerned Scientists report, 2008.

Food Professionals
Chefs
Chefs Collaborative. See www.chefscollaborative.org.

Wolfgang Puck. "Changing Tastes," *Newsweek,* May 7, 2007.

Restaurateurs
Alice Waters: Susan Ives, "Feeding Hearts and Minds," *Land and People* 11 (2) (1999): 29 32.

Vertical integration: Olivia Wu, "Digging Biodynamic," *San Francisco Chronicle,* May 30, 2007. See also Harlan Clifford, Interview with Tod Murphy, *Orion,* May/June, 2007.

Urban Agriculture
Added Value Farm and Growing Power: Tracie McMillan, "Urban Farmers' Crops Go from Vacant Lot to Market," *New York Times,* May 7, 2008.

Kids plant their own pumpkin patch: Linda Riebel, "Urban Gardeners Engage in Pumpkin Planting with their Kids," Examiner.com, http://exm.nr/hdDkvQ.

Master Gardeners
Volunteering: USDA National Institute of Food and Agriculture, "Horticulture More than a Hobby," www.csrees.usda.gov/newsroom/impacts/04index/horticulture.html. This is the only document that I could no longer locate when I was reconfirming websites.

Good food—pass it on: California Foundation for Agriculture in the Classroom, www. cfaitc.org.

Beekeepers
Urban beekeepers: Katherine Harmon, "Urban Beekeepers Keep Cities Abuzz with Pollinators," *Scientific American,* March, 2009. See also Niki Stojnic, "Buzz Kill: Can Urban Beekeepers Save the World?" *Common Ground* (July, 2007): 60-63.

Farmers
Average age of farmers: USDA, "2007 Census of Agriculture, Farmers by Age," www. agcensus.usda.gov/Publications/2007/Online_Highlights/Fact_Sheets/farmer_age.pdf.

Military veterans: Janet Fletcher, "Farmers Recruit Combat Veterans," *San Francisco Chronicle,* September 24, 2008. See www.farmvetco.org and http://ncta.unl.edu/web/ncta/CombatCowboyBoots.

Artisanal creameries: Marian Burros, "The Dairies Are Half-Pint, but the Flavor Isn't," *New York Times,* February 20, 2008.

Food Pro Smorgasbord
Off-beat careers. Ilana DeBare, "These Firms are Bite-Sizing," *San Francisco Chronicle,* July 29, 2007.

The town that was saved by food: Marian Burros, "Uniting Around Food to Save an Ailing Town," *New York Times,* October 8, 2008.

Growing Your Food

Jo Murphy: "Eggplants, Activism Crop Up at Wellesley," *Wellesley Alumnae Magazine*, Fall, 2007; also personal communication.

Kids outstanding in their field: "The Organic Movement," *Roots & Shoots Newsletter* 27 (Fall-Winter, 2006): 8-9.

Why Grow Food?

Victory gardens: Ron Sullivan and Joe Eaton, "The Victory Garden Sprouts Anew," *San Francisco Chronicle*, July 23, 2008.

Sensible investment: Marian Burros, "Banking on Gardening," *New York Times*, June 11, 2008; See also Anne Marie Chaker, "The Vegetable Patch Takes Root," *Wall Street Journal*, June 5, 2008.

70% of households garden: National Gardening Association, "Garden Market Research: Lawn and Garden Sales Up 3 Percent to More than $35 Billion in 2007," www.gardenresearch.com/index.php?q=show&id=2989

Where to Grow

California school gardens: Sabine Muscat, "Bringing Green to Urban Schools," *San Francisco Chronicle*, August 6, 2007.

Brooklyn roof farm: Marian Burros, "Urban Farming, a Bit Closer to the Sun," *New York Times*, June 17, 2009.

The perk that grows on you: Kim Severson, "The Rise of Company Gardens," *New York Times*, May 12, 2010. See also Kim Palmer, "Growth Opportunity," *Minneapolis-St.Paul Star Tribune*, July 17, 2009,

www.startribune.com/lifestyle/homegarden/51024822.html?elr=KArks:DCiU1OiP:Dii UiD3aPc:_Yyc:aULPQL7PQLanchO7DiUr.

Messiah College: Messiah News, "Sustainability Efforts at Messiah College Celebrated in 'Green Awakenings' Report by Renewal," http://blogs.messiah.edu/news_releases/2010/mc-022-10.

Presidents' Climate Commitment: "Signatory List by Institution Name," www.presidentsclimatecommitment.org/signatories/list.

Northland College: "Food for Thought," www.northland.edu/sustainability-campus-initiatives-food-systems.htm.

Food from the fringe: Matthew Green, "San Francisco's Farmland," *San Francisco Chronicle*, October 4, 2008.

Getting Help

Gardening coach: Christina Gillham, "Put Me in (The Garden), Coach," *Newsweek*, February 10, 2008.

"Remote-controlled backyard gardening": Kim Severson, "A Locally Grown Diet With Fuss But No Muss," *New York Times*, July 22, 2008.

Andy Snow. Personal communication.

Veggies in the city: See www.newrootsurbanfarm.org/

Nurture capital: Woody Tasch, "In Soil We Trust," Green Money Journal, 19 (2) (2010): 5, 7, & 17. See also www.slowmoney.org/about.html.

Spice Up Your Social Life

Slow Food: See www.slowfoodusa.org.

National Gardening Association: See www.garden.org.

Underground food economy: Linda Riebel, "Urban Foragers and Citizen Harvesters," The Examiner, July 1, 2010. www.examiner.com http://exm.nr/cVvpDA.

Part V Food for Thought

"Most of the things worth doing": See www.brandeis.edu/givingto/annualfund/jbs.html.

Dueling Data: Trade-offs and the Learning Curve

Livestock diversity threatened: Andrew Rice, "A Dying Breed," New York Times, January 28, 2008.

Organic's success: Michael Pollan, "The Organic Industrial Complex," New York Times, May 13, 2001.

Biofuels: Timothy Searchinger et al., "Use of U.S. Croplands for Biofuels Increases Greenhouse Gases Through Emissions from Land-Use Changes," Science 319 (February 7, 2008): 1238-1240.

Chemicals not tested: Mark Fischetti, "The Great Chemical Unknown," Scientific American, October, 2010. See also Environmental Defense, http://notaguineapig.org/page.cfm?tagID=57051.

The Learning Curve

Catch shares: Environmental Defense Special Report, "Turning the Tide: Fishermen Embrace a New Approach to End Overfishing"(Fall, 2010). See also sustainingfisheries.com and "'Catch Shares' Transform a Troubled Fishery," Solutions 39 (2) (2008): 9, www.edf.org/documents/7744_0408_Solutions.pdf. Also "New Life for a West Coast Fishery," Solutions 39 (4) (2008): 7, www.edf.org/documents/8225_Solutions_0808.pdf. Also Christopher Costello et al., "Can Catch Shares Prevent Fisheries Collapse?" Science 321 (September 19, 2008): 1678-1681. See also "One-Year Review Shows Major Success of Catch Share Program as a Model for Recovering Fisheries," environmentaldefense.org/pressrelease.cfm?content ID=7482. Also Environmental Defense report "Sustaining America's Fishers and Fishing Communities" (2007).

The man in between: David Mas Masumoto, "Married to Walmart: What Was I Thinking?" The Atlantic, June 28, 2010, www.theatlantic.com/food/archive/2010/06/married-to-walmart-what-was-i-thinking/58839.

You Be the Judge

Food-wrapping film: Mark Jewell, "Green Plastics Find Cautious Market," Associated Press, October 22, 2007. See also Morgan Kelly-Pittsburgh, "Plant Plastics Not So Green After All?" 2010, www.futurity.org/earth-environment/plant-plastics-not-so-green-after-all.

Soybeans: Charlotte Vallaeys et al., "Behind the Bean: The Heroes and Charlatans of the Natural and Organic Soy Foods Industry," Cornucopia Institute, 2009 [Executive Summary], www.cornucopia.org/2009/05/soy-report-and-scorecard.

Help Endangered Species
41,000 species worldwide: International Union for Conservation of Nature, http://iucn. org.

RAFT, 1,000 threatened food plants and animals: Gary Paul Nabhan, *Renewing America's Food Traditions* (White River Junction, VT: Chelsea Green, 2008).

Imported
Palm oil: Rainforest Action Network, "Problem with Palm Oil Factsheet," 2010, www. ran.org/content/problem-palm-oil-factsheet. See also Greenpeace, "United Plantations Certified Despite Gross Violations of RSPO Standards," 2008, www.greenpeace.org/ usa/en/media-center/reports/united-plantations-certified-d.

Sea life
Loss of diversity: Boris Worm et al., "Impacts of Biodiversity Loss on Ocean Ecosystem Services," *Science* 314 (November 3, 2006): 787-790.

All creatures near and far: See www.oaklandzoo.org/conservation-programs.

Animal Farm
CAFOs: Doug Gurian-Sherman, "CAFOs Uncovered: The Untold Costs of Confined Animal Feeding Operations," Union of Concerned Scientists report, 2008. Melanie Joy, *Why We Love Dogs, Eat Pigs, and Wear Cows* (San Francisco: Conari Press, 2010); Jeffrey Moussaieff Masson, *The Face on Your Plate: The Truth about Food* (New York: W. W. Norton, 2009). Also Joby Warrick, "Modern Meat: A Brutal Harvest. They Die Piece by Piece," *Washington Post,* April 10, 2001. See also Humane Society of the United States, "'No Battery Hens' Campaign Exposes The Hard-Boiled Truth About Laying Hens," www.hsus.org/farm/camp/nbe/?print=t. See also Diane DeLouzor-Dan, "At Our Mercy: The Eating of Animals," *In Defense of Animals,* 3 (2000): 20-22. Humane Society of the United States, "A Brief Guide to Egg Carton Labels and Their Relevance to Animal Welfare," 2009, www.humanesociety.org/issues/confinement_farm/facts/ guide_egg_labels.html. Also Gene and Lorri Bauston, "Brutality: Main Crop of Factory Farms?" *Earthsave: Healthy People, Healthy Planet.* 10 (3) (1999): 1. Michael W. Fox, *Eating with Conscience: The Bioethics of Food* (Troutdale, OR: New Sage Press, 1997). See also Humane Society of the United States, "An HSUS Report: The Welfare of Animals in the Meat, Egg, and Dairy Industries" 2010, www.humanesociety.org/assets/ pdfs/farm/welfare_overview.pdf.

American Humane Certified: American Humane Association, "The Humane Touch," http://thehumanetouch.org.

Some good news
Cage-free egg market growing: Humane Society of the United States, "Consumers, Companies, Science Favor Cage-Free Eggs," October 27, 2010, www.humanesociety. org /news/press_releases/2010/10/movement_growing_102710.html.

Grass-fed: Jo Robinson, "Grass-Fed Basics," 2010, www.eatwild.com/basics.html.

American Humane Certified: http://TheHumaneTouch.org.

Kleinpeter Farms: "American Humane Certified Producer Profiles," http://thehumanetouch.org/certified-producers/profiles#kleinpeter.

The Nutrition-Industrial Complex
Food share of income: U.S. Bureau of Labor Statistics, "Consumer Expenditures in 2008," March, 2010, http://stats.bls.gov/cex/csxann08.pdf. See also USDA Economic Research Service, "FOOD CPI and Expenditures: Table 7," June 17, 2008,

www.ers.usda.gov/briefing/CPIFoodandExpenditures/Data/table7.htm.

$1 trillion: Economic Research Service of the USDA, "Food CPI and Expenditures," August 25, 2010, www.ers.usda.gov/Briefing/CPIFoodAndExpenditures.

Four meatpacking firms: Eric Schlosser, *Fast Food Nation: The Dark Side of the All-American Meal* (New York: Houghton Mifflin, 2001), 137-139.

Sysco: Ulrich Boser, "Every Bite You Take: How Sysco Came to Monopolize Most of What You Eat," *Slate*, February 21, 2007, www.slate.com/id/2160284.

Industry actions: Marion Nestle, *Food Politics: How The Food Industry Influences Nutrition and Health* (Berkeley, CA: University of California Press, 2002). Michele Simon, *Appetite for Profit: How The Food Industry Undermines Our Health–And How to Fight Back* (New York: Avalon, 2006).

Food Safety

Causes: Felicia Nestor and Wenonah Hauter, "The Jungle 2000: Is America's Meat Fit to Eat?" (Washington, DC: Public Citizen, 2000), www.citizen.org/documents/The-Jungle2000.PDF.

Salmonella outbreak of 2008: Larry Margasa, "How Food Industry Lobbying Slowed Salmonella Search," *San Francisco Chronicle*, July 26, 2008.

"Our food system is broken": Marian Burros, "Who's Watching What We Eat?" *New York Times*, May 16, 2007.

Advertising and Public Relations

$1.6 billion. Adam Voiland, "10 Things the Food Industry Doesn't Want You to Know," *U.S. News and World Report*, October 17, 2008.

"Share of mind." Diane E. Levin and Susan Linn, "The Commercialization of Childhood: Understanding the Problem and Finding Solutions," in Tim Kasser and Allen Kanner (Eds.), *Psychology and Consumer Culture* (Washington, DC: American Psychological Association, 2004).

Public relations: Sheldon Rampton and John Stauber, *Trust Us, We're Experts! How Industry Manipulates Science and Gambles with Your Future* (New York: J.P. Tarcher/Putnam, 2001).

"The denial machine": Sharon Begley, "The Truth about Denial," *Newsweek*, August 13, 2007, 21-29.

"An impediment to public health": The Alliance for Food and Farming, "The Real Dangers of 'Dirty' Produce Lists," www.safefruitsandveggies.com. According to Source Watch (a project of the Center for Media and Democracy), this Alliance is a front group for the fruit and vegetable industry, www.sourcewatch.org/index.php?title=Alliance_for_Food_and_Farming. See also Barry Estabrook, "When Big Ag Attacks: Government-Sponsored Pesticide Propaganda, November 4, 2010, www.theatlantic.com/food/archive/2010/11/when-big-ag-attacks-government-sponsored-pesticide-propaganda/66083.

Lobbying and Co-opting Legislators

Country-of-Origin Labeling Law: "Origins of Our Food," Editorial, *New York Times*, July 4, 2007.

Workplace injury reporting: Roger Horowitz, "The Jungle 2008: Government Manipulates Data on Workers Injuries at Slaughterhouses," 2008, www.organicconsumers.org/articles/article_12659.cfm.

Weakening the regulatory agency: Dina Cappiello, "EPA Tells Staff Don't Talk to Investigators, Press," Associated Press, July 28, 2008.

Business can be green—they've proved it: http://media.patagonia.com/fb/environmental-initiatives-2010/index.html.

Undermining Free Speech
Sugar Association: Elizabeth Querna, "No, It's Not Just Your Sweet Tooth," *U.S. News & World Report*, March 28, 2005.

Spying. Eric Schlosser, "Burger With a Side of Spies," *New York Times,* May 7, 2008.

Hormone-free milk label: Jeff Deasy, "A Major Legal Victory in the Fight for Hormone-Free Milk," *Alternet*, October 19, 2010.

Why Do They Do All This?
Philip Zimbardo, *The Lucifer Effect: Understanding How Good People Turn Evil* (New York: Random House, 2008).

The Positive Side of Big Business
Walmart local sourcing: "Wal-Mart to Source More Local Produce," *GreenBiz,* July 1, 2008, www.greenbiz.com/news/2008/07/01/wal-mart-source-more-local-produce.

Makower's Paradox: Ilana deBare, "Buying Public Is Becoming More at Ease with Renewable Products," *San Francisco Chronicle*, October 12, 2008.

Good Intentions

Fair Trade.
Andrew Downie, "Fair Trade in Bloom," *New York Times,* October 2, 2007. See also Lauren Wilcox, "Going with the Grain," *Smithsonian*, September, 2007.

Sweet success: Jill Santopietro, "When Chocolate is a Way of Life," *New York Times,* November 5, 2008.

Vegetarianism
American Dietetic Association: "Position of the American Dietetic Association: Vegetarian Diets," *Journal of the American Dietetic Association* 109 (7) (2009): 1266-1282, www.eatright.org/about/content.aspx?id=8357.

Eating Lightly for the Earth
Larger portions: Editors, "Obesity: Portions Out of Proportion," *Harvard Women's Health Watch*, 7 (12) (2000): 1.

Overeating an environmental issue: Linda Riebel, "Consuming the Earth: Eating Disorders and Ecopsychology," *Journal of Humanistic Psychology* 41 (2) (2001): 38-58.

3,800 calories a day: USDA, *Agriculture Fact Book 2001-2002,* 14. See also Center for Science in the Public Interest, "Why It's Hard to Eat Well and Be Active in America Today," at www.cspinet.org/nutritionpolicy/food_advertising.html.

"Diseases of dietary excess": Worldwatch Institute, *State of the World* (New York: W.W. Norton, 2000), 71.

Obese by 2030: Y. Wang et al., "Will All Americans Become Overweight or Obese? Estimating the Progression and Cost of the U.S. Obesity Epidemic," *Obesity* 16 (10) (2008): 2323-2330 [Abstract].

Many causes of obesity: Kim Hiatt, Linda Riebel, and Harris Friedman, "The Gap Between What We Know and What We Do About Childhood Obesity: A Multi-Factor Model for Assessment, Intervention, and Prevention," *Journal of Social, Behavioral, and Health Sciences 1* (1) (2007): 1-44. Online at www.jsbhs.org/9049_24322.htm.

Food scientists: David Kessler *The End of Overeating: Taking Control of the Insatiable American Appetite* (New York: Rodale Books, 2009).

Time and Money
"Small changes in our lives": Interview with Environmental Defense, June 13, 2007, www.edf.org/article.cfm?contentID=6486.

The Win-Win-Win Situation
"All over the world": Donella H. Meadows, Dennis L. Meadows, and Jorgen Randers, *Beyond the Limits: Confronting Global Collapse, Envisioning a Sustainable Future* (White River Junction, VT: Chelsea Green, 1992), 209.

Index

CPSIA information can be obtained at www.ICGtesting.com
Printed in the USA
LVOW041705010812

292532LV00012B/14/P